Managing Effectively
Through Tough Times

MASON A. CARPENTER

M. Keith Weikel Professor in Leadership
Department of Management & Human Resources
Wisconsin School of Business
University of Wisconsin-Madison

Prentice Hall

Boston   Columbus   Indianapolis   New York   San Francisco   Upper Saddle River
Amsterdam   Cape Town   Dubai   London   Madrid   Milan   Munich   Paris   Montreal   Toronto
Delhi   Mexico City   Sao Paulo   Sydney   Hong Kong   Seoul   Singapore   Taipei   Tokyo

Acquisition Editors: Kim Norbuta, Jennifer M. Collins
Editorial Director: Sally Yagan
Editor in Chief: Eric Svendsen
Product Development Manager: Ashley Santora
Director of Marketing: Patrice Lumumba Jones
Marketing Manager: Nikki Jones
Marketing Assistant: Susan Osterlitz
Permissions Manager: Charles Morris
Senior Managing Editor: Judy Leale
Senior Operations Specialist: Arnold Vila
Senior Art Director: Janet Slowik
Cover Designer: Karen Quigley
Cover Photo: Bruno Budrovic/SIS/GettyImages, Inc.
Manager, Rights and Permissions: Zina Arabia
Manager, Visual Research: Beth Brenzel
Image Permission Coordinator: Fran Toepfer
Composition: GGS Higher Education Resources, A Division of Premedia Global, Inc.
Full-Service Project Management: Jeanine Furino/GGS Higher Education Resources,
    A Division of Premedia Global, Inc.
Printer/Binder: Courier/Kendallville
Typeface: Minion 10/12

Credits and acknowledgments borrowed from other sources and reproduced, with
permission, in this textbook appear on appropriate page within text.

Pearson Prentice Hall™ is a trademark of Pearson Education, Inc.
Pearson® is a registered trademark of Pearson plc
Prentice Hall® is a registered trademark of Pearson Education, Inc.

Pearson Education Ltd., London
Pearson Education Singapore, Pte. Ltd
Pearson Education, Canada, Inc.
Pearson Education–Japan
Pearson Education Australia PTY,
    Limited
Pearson Education North Asia, Ltd., Hong Kong
Pearson Educación de Mexico, S.A. de C.V.
Pearson Education Malaysia, Pte. Ltd
Pearson Education Upper Saddle River, New Jersey

Prentice Hall
is an imprint of

10 9 8 7 6 5 4 3 2 1
ISBN-13: 978-0-13-702504-6
ISBN-10:   0-13-702504-1

www.pearsonhighered.com

A Short Note from the Author

Dear Colleague,

I am hopeful that you will find this supplement—*Managing Effectively Through Tough Times*—to be timely, interesting, and relevant. In partnership with my publisher Pearson Education, I wrote this supplement for professors, managers, and students alike, with the aim of reminding them about what they learned (or should have learned) in business school. While harsh economic times, like those that we are experiencing around the globe today, present managers with tough choices, such times also provide a great opportunity to get back to the basics and position the firm for better things to come. However, it is relatively easy (unfortunately) for managers to take actions now that contribute to survival but actually get in the way of future success. The purpose of this supplement is to shed some light on the managerial choices that may help organizations avoid this pitfall.

This supplement strives to provide an action playbook for managing effectively through tough times. Specifically, you will learn how managers can look to eight areas for clues to the key survival tactics needed today that also contribute to the achievement of prosperity (and competitive advantage) tomorrow. Following an introductory vignette on the challenges and opportunities experienced by Starbucks, I walk through the following set of action items: (1) Look at your compass—understand and communicate the roots and deep meaning behind your mission and vision; (2) Get back to your strategy—strategy is about choice, what you do and don't do; (3) Get closer to your customers—know what delights them and what causes them pain (and perhaps get rid of a few); (4) Invest in human capital—the people make the place; (5) Leverage social capital—social capital is the resources available in and through personal and business relationships; understand and manage it; (6) Understand what drives innovation and change—cultivate the DNA for change; (7) Preserve financial capital—master the cause-and-effect relationships behind the balance sheet and income statement (that is, develop an understanding of the concepts behind a balanced scorecard and strategy map); and, (8) Practice values-based leadership—tough times can bring out the best, and sometimes the worst, in people; don't leave this to chance.

Beyond the valuable real-world lessons outlined in each of the eight sections, I am also hopeful that it is clear that two biases—a bias for *action* and a bias for *optimism*—weave all the sections of the supplement together. My students have taught me the value of learning through experience (a bias for action) and, without optimism, we are unlikely to take the actions needed to learn.

Onward and upward,

Mason A. Carpenter
M. Keith Weikel Professor in Leadership

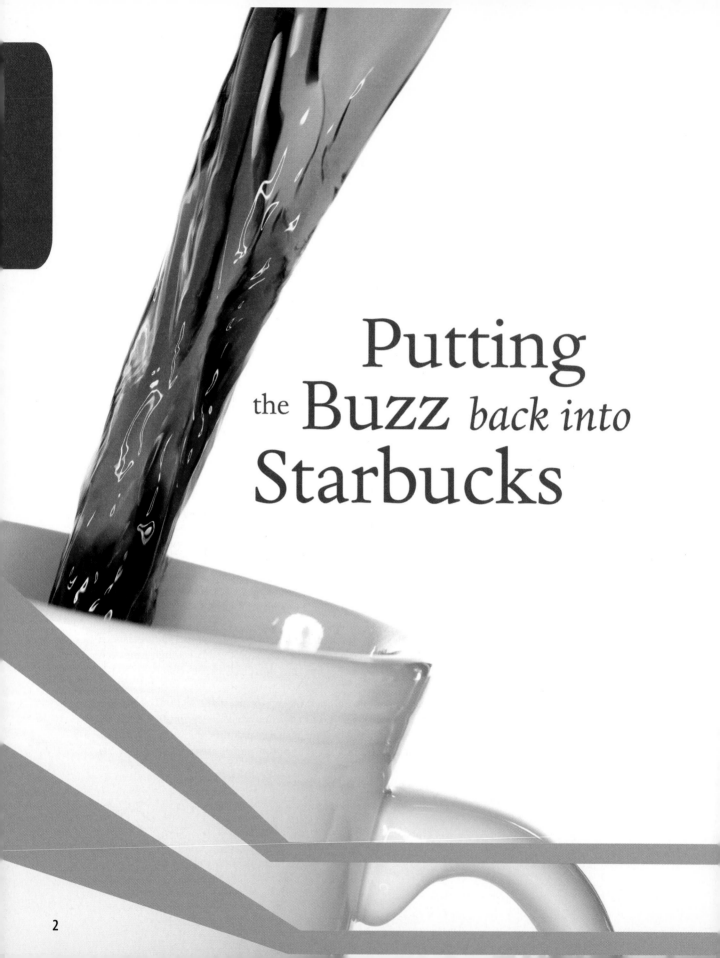

Putting the Buzz back into Starbucks

$\mathcal{G}$oing into the U.S. presidential elections in 2008, most Americans had a sense that their country's economic situation was a bit shaky. Although the government declared in December 2008 that the U.S. economy had officially entered into a recession in December 2007, the economic downturn had been beginning to take a toll in the months before that.

Starbucks, the global coffee experience purveyor, was but one data point among many which suggested that greater pain lay ahead. For example, Starbucks' fourth quarter 2008 profits had plummeted an alarming 97 percent. The precipitous drop seemed mostly due to costs associated with closing hundreds of stores and did not appear to be a trend. Still, after WaMu's sale to JPMorgan Chase earlier in October 2008, and with the economy in the emergency room, a fall like that was more than unnerving.

The trials and tribulations of Starbucks provide a useful lens for looking at the challenges of managing effectively through tough times. While all changes don't necessarily start at the top, many do, and the challenges at Starbucks are no exception: The company's CEO was let go, and Howard Schultz, co-founder and chairman of the board, installed as new CEO. In many ways, this episode in Starbucks' history can be characterized as going back to go forward—that is, returning to the organization's core business and rallying the troops (its employees and customers) around the community that makes Starbucks likely to be a survivor in better times.

As with most other firms in today's tough time, the future of Starbucks is uncertain, but there is ample room for optimism. Starbucks' legacy will be written by the actions taken in the months and years to come. But it is punctuated by the return of co-founder Howard Schultz to the position of CEO in December 2007 and his dialogue with the employees (Starbucks *partners*) that make Starbucks the enviable and trendsetting bundle of products and experience that launched a new industry.

In a continuing series of letters to Starbucks' partners (essentially all internal and external stakeholders), Schultz lays out the challenges and opportunities facing Starbucks going forward. These letters, the first three of which are summarized below, provide valuable insights into the change processes embraced by Starbucks, as well as glimpses into the company's past and future.

Transformation Agenda Communication #1 January 7, 2008. In the first letter Schultz opens with a discussion of the history of Starbucks and how this history was punctuated by the June 19, 1992 IPO when the company had only 119 stores. (At the time this letter was written, Starbucks had grown to 15,000 stores and operated in 43 countries.) In the letter Schultz notes a key transition point—when the Starbucks' board named him to replace incumbent CEO Jim Donald. Schultz says, *"Johnson was a passionate and tireless advocate for Starbucks, and his contribution to our company cannot be overstated . . . We are fortunate, though, that the challenge we face is one of our own making. Because of this, we know what needs to be done to ensure our long-term future success around the world."*[1]

In addition to the leadership changes, Schulz laid out the following goals of his *transformation agenda.*

- Improving the current state of the U.S. business.

- Reigniting Starbucks emotional attachment to its customers by restoring the connection customers have with the company, the coffee, the brand, and the stores.

- Realigning the Starbucks organization and streamlining the management of the organization to better support customer-focused initiatives by ensuring that the company's support and planning functions are most effectively dedicated to the customer experience.

- Expanding its presence around the world, by building a profitable business outside the United States and capitalizing on the enormous untapped potential for the Starbucks brand.

Schulz concludes his first letter with a statement that Starbucks is well positioned to navigate these uncertain times. *"In the meantime,"* Schultz adds, *"I want to thank you for your dedication to Starbucks and for your commitment to earning the trust of our customers every day. Our success is up to us. We know what we need to do to win, and we will do it. Onward, Howard"*

Transformation Agenda Communication #2 January 11, 2008. In his second letter to Starbucks partners, issued just days after his first letter, Schultz announced the new leadership team. Beyond many major changes in responsibilities, former Starbucks executives were brought back on board to reignite internal attention to the Starbucks brand. Specifically, *"Harry Roberts, a former Starbucks executive, is returning to the company as senior vice president and chief creative officer. In this newly created role, Roberts and his team will be responsible for the customer in-store experience, including creative expression, merchandise strategy and the overall 'look and feel' of the company's stores."*[2]

Transformation Agenda Communication #3 January 30, 2008. Schulz reported that the three-pronged transformation agenda for Starbucks was well underway: (1) Starbucks would improve the current state of its U.S. business, (2) reignite the emotional attachment with its customers and, (3) make foundational changes for the long term. In the 30 days since the first letter from Schultz, Starbucks had already slowed the pace of U.S. store openings and closed underperforming stores. At the same time the company ramped up its international store openings and accelerated plans to further international expansion. Product offerings like warmed breakfast sandwiches were cut, and future product offerings were judged solely on how well they complemented Starbucks stronghold in superior coffee and espresso beverages. Beyond these actions already in progress, Schultz announced two new training initiatives. The first was an investment in training retail partners (employees) with an aim of providing them with the tools and resources needed to exceed customer expectations. The second ordered the return of the "Leadership Conference," a forum for store managers that would not only provide a basis for career development but would provide another vehicle for building understanding of Starbucks' vision and strategy.[3]

Onward At Starbucks' biennial stock analyst conference in December 2008, Schultz and other executives provided an update on the company's progress and outlook. Schultz opened the conference with an affirmation of Starbucks' core mission and values. In terms of the Starbucks specific operating approach during these tough times, Shultz outlined an operating approach that included maintaining the loyalty of core customers through continued innovation and rewards, raising the bar on operational excellence, and taking an aggressive approach to cost savings. "The entire retail sector is operating in a very tough economic environment. While Starbucks has not been immune to the decline in consumer confidence, we are fortunate to have a world-class brand and a loyal customer base," said Schultz. "In this environment, it is critical to put our feet in the shoes of our customers."[4] Schultz commented further, "We generate strong cash flow, have solid liquidity and are executing rigorous cost-containment initiatives to improve our bottom line. Starbucks will continue to take actions to improve our U.S. business and take advantage of targeted growth opportunities in high potential markets. Integral to this are our efforts to elevate the Starbucks Experience and staying true to our core values. This focus will help us emerge stronger, more efficient and better able to deliver value to our shareholders over the long term."<<<

Introduction

As the U.S. financial meltdown continued unabated in late November 2008, U.S. Treasury Secretary Henry Paulson stated, "There is no playbook for responding to turmoil we have never before faced."[5] Such statements, and the continuing financial woes of such admired companies as Starbucks served to further roil the already-fragile global financial markets and offered little consolation to the managers tasked with leading their organizations effectively through uncertain and tough times.

But what does it mean to *manage effectively through tough times*? Is there really no playbook for managers to follow? Of course, there is a managerial playbook—well, to paraphrase Jack Sparrow from the blockbuster movie *Pirates of the Caribbean*, the playbook provides managers with *guidelines* and not simple rules that can be followed blindly (if you've seen the movie, you know that it turned out that the pirates' code was like a set of guidelines)—even for managers in companies facing the most dire of circumstances. Some of these guidelines-in-action are seen in the companies profiled in Jim Collins's business best sellers, *Good to Great* (2001) and *Built to Last* (1994, with Jerry Porras).[6] Still other valuable insights are found in Jeff Pfeffer's uncompromising *What Were They Thinking?* (2007).[7] While salvation is never guaranteed, there is indeed an orchestrated set of steps that managers can take to better their position and that of their firm.

For some organizations, effective management will make the difference between death and survival. For other firms, effective management will position their organizations to emerge from the global downturn alive—with greater focus, clearer purpose, and brighter future prospects. After all, in Chinese, the word for *crisis* is written using two characters: The first represents danger, and the second stands for opportunity. Similarly, according to a number of studies by the strategy consulting firm McKinsey & Company, "Some companies emerge from a recession stronger and more highly valued than they were before the economy soured. By making strategic choices that sometimes defy conventional wisdom, they increase their stock market valuations relative to those of their former peers and thus gain more power to shape their industries."[8] Private and family-run businesses have similar opportunities.

Admittedly, an organization needs to survive current challenges in order to prosper later. However, it is relatively easy (unfortunately) for managers to take actions today that contribute to survival but actually get in the way of future success. In some cases, such as cutting R&D or customer service, that might be obvious, but in other cases, such as making across-the-board cuts or reducing investments in training or technology, it might not be so obvious. However, all these actions can have disastrous long-term effects. Even if they're not disastrous, they do not put the firm in an advantageous position when good times return. The purpose of this supplement is to help you understand the managerial choices that help organizations avoid this pitfall. Specifically, you will learn how managers can link survival tactics needed today to the achievement of prosperity tomorrow.

EIGHT AREAS TO CONSIDER

These are certainly challenging times, and not for the faint of heart. The path forward involves attention to detail in eight fundamental areas. These eight areas, spanning all activities in the organization, are summarized in Figure 1. Not all firms will need to make changes in all areas, and managers will want to start with the low-hanging fruit. There is also, of course, the reality that some changes will be more urgent than others. For example, a business that is running out of cash will likely have to focus on the financial dimension for changes in order for any of the other dimensions to matter. However, as a word of caution, experience has shown that *urgency* and *importance* are often confused in terms of setting managerial priorities.

Figure 1 Be Mindful of These Eight Areas

Source: Mason A. Carpenter.

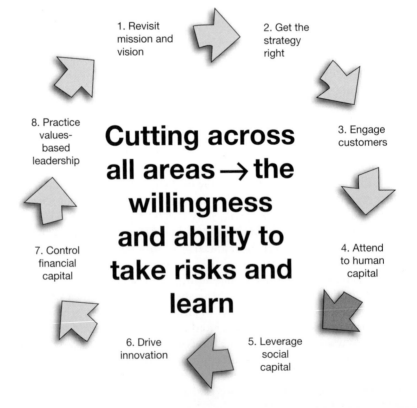

1. Revisit mission and vision
2. Get the strategy right
3. Engage customers
4. Attend to human capital
5. Leverage social capital
6. Drive innovation
7. Control financial capital
8. Practice values-based leadership

Cutting across all areas → the willingness and ability to take risks and learn

Cutting across each of the eight areas is the need for management to have or develop the capacity, willingness, and ability to take risks and to learn. (Both taking risks and learning are essential but much easier said than done.) Similarly, you will quickly see how each area is somewhat dependent on the status of other areas, so in that sense, managers who are able to manage effectively through tough times do so in a deliberate yet systemic fashion. Let's briefly look at these eight areas in turn and then dive more deeply into each one.

Revisit Mission and Vision

As summarized in Figure 1, managers start this journey—in this supplement and in their organization—by revisiting the past. You need to ask whether you and all the others in your organization understand and live the mission and vision.

Get the Strategy Right

Mission and vision are clearly important, but they are not substitutes for strategy. Getting the strategy right is where you need to go next. Strategy is essentially about choice, focus, and priorities—what the organization does (by choice) and what its managers choose not to do. More importantly, strategy is an impetus (not a substitute) for action. Tough times give managers an opportunity to tighten down the strategy by keeping what works and jettisoning what does not.

Engage Customers

On the surface, customer engagement seems intuitive and logical. However, even in good times, many firms have trouble executing well in this area. Such difficulty tends to arise from at least two related missteps. First, the firm's focus on core customer needs can become fuzzy, often as a result of growth during the "good times." Second, as a result of unfocused growth, an organization may be serving customers that are unprofitable or distracting. While it sometimes seem that the solution to tough times is to fire employees (i.e., reduce labor and other costs across the board), it may make more sense to fire some customers who don't fit the strategy and strengths of the firm.

Attend to Human Capital

While it is a good practice to control costs and waste, tough times dictate better internal controls (i.e., it's no longer an option). However, in terms of employees, this often translates into across-the-board employee cuts or hiring freezes. Any such across-the-board moves, unless the firm had a perfect fit between human capital prior to the tough times, indicate that managers have not gotten the strategy right or are ignoring the priorities that the strategy dictates.

Leverage Social Capital

You have probably heard a little about social capital, starting with the old adage that it's *who you know, not what you know*. In some situations, social capital determines what you know (i.e., who managers and employees know influences what they know). Social capital is a result of your social networks, and reflects the resources available in and through personal and business social networks. Such resources include ideas, information, business leads, money, influence, and trust. Whereas an organizational chart might show who reports to whom, an organization's social network is the means by which the organization's work actually gets done. For instance, if this somewhat invisible organizational structure (which does not typically show up on the organizational chart) is not well understood, then any changes made to personnel might unintentionally damage the organization's future prospects.

Drive Innovation and Organizational Change

"Innovate or die." This mantra, popularized by management guru Tom Peters, has been repeated many times—by the media, governments, business leaders, business professors, and consultants.[9] At its core is the need to better understand the organizational processes leading to innovation and adaptability. A recent Max Gladwell blog post observed that "As the financial crisis rips across the economy, it's forcing innovation and adaptation on a scale that should make

Needed—An organizational capacity for *risk taking* and *learning* Throughout this supplement, you will see that a capacity for risk taking and learning are essential to managing effectively in tough times. *Risk-taking* capacity refers to the cultivation of an organizational climate that tolerates risk taking but at the same time is able to quickly minimize downside damage. With *learning* capacity, in contrast, managers factor the causes of wins and losses into doing things differently. Learning organizations exhibit mindful action, not mindless action.

Darwin proud."[10] The challenge and opportunity for managers is to change fast enough in ways that delight customers, pay the bills, and at the same time allow the organization to retain and develop its best people. Yes, change takes care and effort. But, given these tough times, managers need to ask themselves whether there will ever be a better time for operational, service, or product innovation than when business-to-business (B2B) and business-to-consumer (B2C) customers are clearly stretched thin.

Control Financial Capital In financial circles, the saying is that "cash is king." This is particularly true in the case of business turnarounds—that is, where a firm is clearly going broke. In terms of firm survival and longer-term prosperity, however, cash may not be the only celebrity, but it certainly is part of the (eight) royal jewels. Understanding where business is in terms of financial capital requires two sets of related actions. First, management must instill the spirit of turnaround management in everyday activities. Second, managers should develop a clear financial map of how the strategy creates value. This type of map is sometimes called a balanced scorecard, but in the form we are discussing, it is much more than a system of accounting controls. (Judging from the state of the financial services industry, controls are not a bad thing!) Specifically, a financial strategy map should show how the resource allocation decisions underlying the strategy lead to near-term firm survival and longer-term competitive advantage.

Practice Values-based Leadership. To paraphrase Charles Dickens, "tough times bring out the best in people as well as the worst." Tough times put managers in a situation that is new, sometimes unpleasant, and always without a readily clear-cut course of action. When a situation arises that we have to deal with, there are three different ways we can arrive at a decision on what to do: We can use our beliefs to formulate a response, we can use our intuition to formulate a response, or we can use our values to formulate a response. Importantly, beliefs and intuition are based on context (and sometimes panic, in the case of tough times) and past experience. *Values-based leadership* is the action of articulating the wants and needs of employees by helping them understand and act on the company's shared vision.[11] A values-based leader inspires employees by listening and understanding their needs and influencing them to make the necessary changes to accomplish the company's shared vision. If we use our values to make decisions, our decisions will align with the future we want to experience and will not be constrained by the past. Values transcend both contexts and experiences. Values-based leadership is also based in moral values and a consistent display of respect for all followers.[12] Values are becoming the preferred mode of decision making in business. Therefore, it is not surprising to find ample research showing that adaptable and values-driven companies are the most successful organizations on the planet.[13] Values-based leadership helps companies manage effectively in tough times.

Mission and Vision

In some organizations, mission and vision statements are like long-lost distant relatives: out of sight and out of mind. In other businesses, the mission and vision are bound in glossy covers and posted vividly in annual reports and on the company website, yet they are completely disconnected from what management and employees actually do. Which scenario do you think is better—the first, where managers don't pretend to know their firm's mission and vision, or the second, where managers talk a good game but don't actually walk the talk?

Hopefully you answered "none of the above." Neither scenario is desirable. In fact, both scenarios are highly dysfunctional from the standpoint that, absent a clear mission and vision, it is nearly impossible for an organization to formulate and execute a coherent

Figure 2 Mission, Vision, and Strategy

Source: Mason A. Carpenter.

strategy. As summarized in Figure 2, *mission* reflects an organization's reason for being, and *vision* summarizes the organization's future aspirations in terms of what it wants to become. Importantly, mission should subsume and foreshadow vision because the vision emerges from and allows fulfillment of the mission. Because a *strategy* is the expression of how a firm will achieve its mission and vision, fuzzy or absent mission and vision often result in fuzzy or absent strategy. During good times, and even through some tough times, firms can survive without a clear and compelling mission and vision. However, such firms are analogous to a car or plane set to travel using an automatic pilot: At some point, traveling conditions change, and this requires human intervention. Absent a mission and vision, such intervention will be infrequent at best and wrong-headed at worst.

Mission and vision are often crafted and communicated through some form of written statement. Importantly, it is the deeper shared meaning behind these statements that matter most, but any dialogue about such meaning is made easier with some form of written statement. Let's look at how managers can structure the development or review process for mission and vision in a way that builds a solid foundation for the strategies that will be designed to achieve them.

CRAFTING THE MISSION STATEMENT

While there is pretty good evidence that firms with compelling missions and visions perform better than those without them,[14] there is not much systematic guidance as to what they should contain. After all, managers and employees might find the task of stating their business's "reason for being" as being pretty vague and open-ended (or simply "fluffy").

To provide a bit more structure here, this supplement follows some guidelines suggested by professors Richard O'Halloran and David O'Halloran, in their book *The Mission Primer* (1999). Consistent with the overarching and integrative aims of this supplement, O'Halloran and O'Halloran define a mission statement more inclusively than most. Specifically, they say, "a mission statement should describe the fundamental objectives of the business, and as such includes what people variously refer to as mission, values, guiding principles, credos, corporate philosophies, visions, strategic intent, goals, key processes, beliefs, management actions/behaviors, codes of conduct, quality statements, and so on."[15]

One of the most insightful and helpful suggestions that O'Halloran and O'Halloran provide to managers is to formulate a mission statement with the aim of complying with Gast's laws. Walter Gast was a professor at St. Louis University in the 1950s. His "laws" say that competitive advantage will be a function of adequate returns to investors and the production of a useful service or product *in addition to* "increasing the wealth of society, providing productive employment opportunities, helping employees find meaningful and satisfying work, and pay fair wages."[16]

Gast's laws—there are six of them in all—can be summarized as follows:[17]

Law 1: A business must produce a want—a satisfying commodity or service—and continually improve its ability to meet needs.

Law 2: A business must increase the wealth or quality of life of society through the economic use of labor and capital.

Law 3: A business must provide opportunities for the productive employment of people.

Law 4: A business must provide opportunities for the satisfaction of normal occupational desires.

Law 5: A business must provide just wages for labor.

Law 6: A business must provide a just return on capital.

Managers can use Gast's laws as a litmus test for their organizations' mission statements in at least two ways. First, if a manager is just beginning to draft a mission statement, he or she can use the laws as a checklist for what can be included. Brevity is not necessarily the primary goal in drafting mission statements, so managers can go beyond these laws in laying out the key components. For instance, a mission statement might address both environmental impact and social impact, and such concerns would justify their own respective line items. It is, however, a reasonable objective to have the mission and vision statements, together, fit on one printed page (in a reasonable font size!). The second way that Gast's laws can be used is to assess completeness—that is, to ensure that a mission statement really covers all the necessary bases.

Across both these litmus tests, managers will want to make sure that each item in a mission statement is complementary as opposed to being contradictory, and this is where the investment of time in developing a shared understanding of the mission among managers and employees is critical. For example, for many businesses, survival is a function of paying competitive returns to investors (e.g., stockholders, debt holders such as banks). To the extent that environmental and social values are part of the mission (and they should be), the pursuit of those values may require novel and innovative means such that they also yield acceptable returns on capital. The idea behind the use of Gast's laws is that an organization can strive for a balance among competing values, as opposed to the narrow focus on any one or a few to the detriment of others (and the longer-term viability of the organization). The pursuit of balance among mission statement values is well shown in a series of mission statement excerpts from Mars, the family-run and very profitable global food company, shown in Exhibit 1.

CRAFTING A VISION STATEMENT

Mission statements, by communicating core values, also foreshadow future aspirations. For instance, the Mars company talks about it mission in such terms: "At a time when change is constant, and in a business that continues to evolve, our [mission] offers a link with our traditions and a bridge into the future."[19]

While good mission statements do have a future-oriented component, however, a vision statement has the sole objective of capturing what managers want the future of the organization to be. Great vision statements should create anxiety about the status quo and incentive for employees to stretch the organization to realize bigger and better accomplishments each day. At the same time, vision statements can be somewhat ambiguous about the exact

Exhibit 1 The Mission Statement of Mars, Inc.[18]

Mars, Inc., is a $25 billion maker of such worldwide favorites as M&M's, Snickers, and the Mars Bar. Its other confections include 3 Musketeers, Dove, Milky Way, Skittles, Twix, and Starburst sweets; Combos and Kudos snacks; Uncle Ben's rice; and pet food under the names Pedigree, Sheba, and Whiskas. Mars also provides office beverage services and makes beverage vending equipment. Mars executives describe their organization as "a global company with family values."

The Mars mission statement comprises what the company calls its "Five Principles":

Quality—"The consumer is our boss, quality is our work and value for money is our goal."

Responsibility—"As individuals, we demand total responsibility from ourselves; as associates, we support the responsibilities of others."

Mutuality—"A mutual benefit is a shared benefit; a shared benefit will endure."

Efficiency—"We use resources to the full, waste nothing and do only what we can do best."

Freedom—"We need freedom to shape our future; we need profit to remain free."

Source: The copyright and all other rights in Mars's "Five Principles" are owned by Mars, Incorporated. The "Five Principles" are printed with permission of Mars, Incorporated. Mars, Incorporated is not associated with Pearson Prentice Hall. © Mars, Inc. 2009.

nature of progress because many of the specifics underlying how the vision is realized will be spelled out in the firm's strategy and shown in the firm's actions.

Intel, the global technology firm, provides a great example of such a vision statement:

> Intel pushes the boundaries of innovation so our work can make people's lives more exciting, fulfilling, and manageable. And our work never stops. We never stop looking for the next leap ahead—in technology, education, culture, manufacturing, and social responsibility. And we never stop striving to deliver solutions with greater benefits for everyone.[20]

As is the case with Intel, effective vision statements are also distilled down into tagline versions—Intel's tagline for its vision is "innovations that move the world forward." Such taglines are both easy to remember and serve as a constant reminder about the organization's underlying vision. These taglines are discussed and debated regularly within an organization, and they figure prominently in communications and interactions with key stakeholders, such as customers, suppliers, and investors.

In their best-selling book *Built to Last* (1997), authors Collins and Porras note that such taglines are more than window dressing in great companies.[21] They help managers build and steward powerful visions by linking the organization's core ideology with a vivid view of the future. The first half, core ideology, is some capability, or more likely a combination of capabilities, deeply held within the organization, such as Apple's creativity or Hewlett-Packard's ability to innovate. One of the critical factors Collins and Porras note in their research on stellar organizations is that this ideology may be captured in written statements but can't be created by written statements. That is, the capabilities must be real.

The second half, a vivid view of the future, is a function itself of two related pieces. For instance, the picture is made more tangible when the vision moves the organization toward what Collins and Porras call a big, hairy, audacious goal (BHAG). Such goals can be quantitative or qualitative, and they can identify a common enemy, role model, transformation, or some combination of these. For example, Wal-Mart's early BHAG was "to become a $125 billion company by the year 2000." This quantitative goal was very easy to communicate and understand, and it really forced the organization to stretch and innovate.

The fact that the vision might include a clearly articulated BHAG provides the second input into making it vivid: That is, the vision is vibrant, engaging, and specific. One of the clearest examples of such a BHAG characteristic is the goal of NASA in the 1960s of putting a person on the moon. Today, more current examples would include a biotech firm's objective of eliminating a certain form of cancer within the next 25 years. Or, for example, Genentech's vision to attack a broader range of human ailments: "Our vision is to utilize the science of biotechnology to become a leader in revolutionizing the treatment of patients with cancer, immunological diseases and angiogenic disorders."[22] This vision include BHAGs of bringing at least 15 new major products to the market and becoming the number-one U.S. oncology company in sales. The tagline version of Genentech's vision is "in business for life," which, as you can imagine, clearly communicates to stakeholders the core ideology underlying Genentech's mission, vision, and strategy. More recently, SABMiller stated the vision that the company wants to become an *able competitor*—that is, it wants to ably, nimbly, and profitably cause competitive damage to its much-larger rival Anheuser-Busch, parent company of Budweiser beer (sort of like a *Beat Bud* mantra).

WHY NOW?

In good times, mission and vision are often hard to talk about because there is no impetus for change or they are off the daily decision-making radar, in a taken-for-granted fashion. Moreover, good times tend to provide buoyancy to organizational performance, such that managers and employees are insulated from the instrumental and guiding role that activated mission and vision statements can play. In tough times, the collective act of expressly revisiting, reinforcing, or revising the mission and vision can give managers and employees a sense of purpose and control that builds a bridge from the current tough times to better times in the future. Mission and vision serve to refocus and reinvigorate key organizational stakeholders during a time of nearly crisis-level uncertainty.

Strategy

You just read that good strategies are the means by which managers plan and communicate how they will achieve their organization's mission and vision. Importantly, while a clear and compelling mission and vision are essential to good strategizing, they are not a substitute for a good strategy. Good strategies are not only clear and complete, they are clear enough that they serve to guide managers' and employees' daily decisions and actions. That is, managers should be able to translate the implications of the strategy to their Outlook calendars and high-priority "to-do" lists.

Strategies can be mapped to an Outlook calendar when they reflect choices about *where* the firm plans to compete (what product, service, and geographic markets), *how* it competes (some combination of uniqueness, cost, or price, along with choices about using organic, cooperative, or acquisitive strategy vehicles). That is, the strategy fosters action (and no strategy, however compelling, is a substitute for action)! Moreover, if a firm has a clear direction in terms of the where and how, the strategy will also communicate how quickly the firm expects to move forward, along with the signposts that tell managers that the firm is on track. Finally, and this is not being overly simplistic, the strategy should predict (or at least hypothesize) that "if we do X, Y, and Z" then this will be the financial consequences—specifically, the strategy should point to a clear economic logic.

Chipotle, the fast-casual restaurant chain, provides a great example of good strategy in action—a strategy that shows how managers are choosing what to do and what not to do, and a strategy that has clear implications for daily (and longer-term) actions. For example, Chipotle competes primarily in North America, and even there its menu is restricted to wrapped or unwrapped burritos and tacos. The company never advertises a burrito without its foil wrapper because "only you know what is in your perfect burrito."[23] Ingredients are fresh, organic, and of the highest quality. Growth is also organic—that is, Chipotle builds, opens, and owns its own chain of stores, eschewing the familiar franchise-owner model. The pace of growth is kept within the limits of what Chipotle is able to fund through internal means, and new stores are added within existing served markets to take advantage of current strengths and success.

Chipotle is highly profitable, which is one aspect that supports the positive nature of the strategy's economic logic. Perhaps more telling, however, is the way this logic spills over in terms of fundamental operating features. If Chipotle's strategy is one of clear focus—on but a few menu items and a few super-fresh organic ingredients—then these features should play out positively in giving Chipotle faster inventory turns than competitors (think of inventory as "frozen cash" and inventory turns as how long it takes a company to convert its frozen stuff to real cash). Indeed, Chipotle is one of the best in the business at generating pure cash from its fixed and current assets.[24]

For examples of good strategies during tough times (or good strategies period), it is often helpful to visit industries that are in turmoil, regardless of the state of the economy. The U.S. beer industry, for instance, has been flat in terms of units sold and total revenues for about a decade. However, Miller Beer, the subsidiary of global beer giant SABMiller, has been an aggressive, innovative, and able competitor against the still-larger U.S. player Anheuser-Busch. Miller's management has done this by getting closer to its core customers and better defining for them why they should choose Miller beers over those of competitors. At the same time, Miller has been very aggressive in both developing new product offerings and reducing costs in product areas where sales growth is clearly stagnant or negative. Most recently, this dual-pronged strategy of innovation and cost reduction was launched into hyperdrive by the merger of Miller with Molson-Coors (to be called MillerCoors, also a partner with prior parent SABMiller).

Whether you look to Chipotle (in a growth industry, regardless of the state of the economy) or MillerCoors (a relatively stagnant industry, at least in North America), one of the hallmarks of good strategies is a cascading relationship from mission, to vision, to strategy, and then to the ultimate tactical and operating actions that such a cascade implies. In many ways, the nexus between strategic and more tactical or operating decisions can be seen in the form of the various internal projects or initiatives that are under way.

BRIDGING STRATEGY AND TACTICS

Strategy typically comes from top management (top down), while projects are typically started by middle management (bottom up). When top-down strategy is out of alignment with bottom-up projects, the inevitable consequence is either a drag on performance or poor performance. As business advisor Cathleen Benko observes, "fewer than 15% of employees can state their company's strategic goals. If you can't articulate the strategy you can't make smart decisions about which projects to take on. Lack of clarity also leaves lots of room for interpretation of the company's strategy."[25] To combat such myopia, Benko recommends that a firm view and approve projects through some form of "strategy lens"—that is, instead of looking at the strategy for insight about what the firm will look like in three to five years, look at the projects that are under way. After all, the fruition of those projects will be what the firm is really doing. With that type of project inventory in place, managers can then go back and keep, pare, or adjust the project portfolio so that it is in alignment with the actual strategy. While firms must take care not to make such a process too cumbersome, one of the beneficial end results is the development of a project portfolio brain of sorts—that is, a clearinghouse that catalogs all the projects under way at any point in time and maps out their longer-term implications.

Beyond bridging the strategic and the tactical, another benefit of such a project-portfolio approach is that managers might be able to break down the biggest and most complex projects into smaller pieces, or chunks. This approach can help the firm assess and evaluate the merits and progress of each piece. It does not preclude projects that are outside the scope of the current strategy. However, it does mean that managers identify these peripheral projects, note that they are experiments, and cite the results of the experiment that might help the firm with its current or future strategy. Moreover, if the smaller projects need to be approved based on demonstrable positive results, then those incremental benefits will accrue to the organization much more quickly.

At Carlson Hospitality Worldwide, this part-and-parcel approach is referred to as *chunking*. The general notion of chunking is summarized in Figure 3. "Chunking helps us learn constantly and perpetually reassess our priorities," says Carlson executive Scott Heintzeman. "It also reduces risk and focuses people's efforts on each work unit. And because the work on each chunk extends for no more than three to six months, people maintain their energy and enthusiasm."[26]

Finally, because a project portfolio helps align projects with strategy, when cuts are completely necessary, the firm's managers will be making informed choices about which projects to keep, cut, or postpone. This may sound intuitive, but, increasingly, firms rely on consultants and contract employees to operate their businesses and steward the development and execution of strategy-critical projects. While this practice provides a sometimes effective way for firms to efficiently and effectively manage scarce internal human capital, the unfortunate byproduct is that such "temp" workers are often the first to be let go during tough times. Thus, in an effort to preserve the jobs of non-temporary employees, management may be inadvertently cutting the flow of blood to the essential projects that would really provide those employees (and the company) with a viable competitive future.

Figure 3 Using a Project Mind-set to Bridge Strategy and Tactics

Source: Mason A. Carpenter.

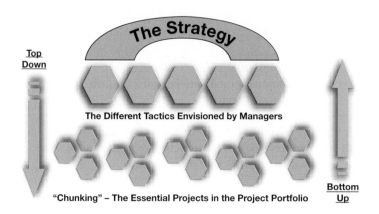

WHY NOW?

In good times, many firms have the challenge of managing "scope creep," or the launch of so many new initiatives that there is no realistic way of keeping up with them. Similarly, for a few firms, in good times the greatest threat is that their growth will outstrip their available resources, be they human, financial, or logistical. Strategy is critical in tough times for reasons similar to these. First, any cutbacks in projects or resources should mirror the organization's priorities; the strategy should dictate these priorities. Perhaps more importantly, in tough times organizations, managers, and employees run the acute risk of succumbing to *threat rigidity*—a restriction of information and constriction of perceived control.[27] Rosabeth Kanter describes this in its darkest human form as the psychology of distress that "causes managers to dislike and avoid one another, hide information, and deny responsibility."[28] Such an effect on information flow and perception of control impedes effective decision making. Indeed, research suggests that decision-making effectiveness in uncertain environments is dependent on managers' ability to utilize more information, create systems to promote debate and information sharing, and use a decentralized method of control over decision-making processes.[29]

Customers

How many managers would say that customers do not matter? Of course they matter! After all, directly and indirectly, customers pay the company's bills. In the extreme case, where the nature of the organization and its leaders' relationships with employees and customers is turned on its head (as compared to the traditional view), it is the partnership between the firm and its customers where value is created. This contemporary view of the customer-individualized company, inspired by business thought-leaders Sumantra Ghoshal and Chris Bartlett, is summarized in Figure 4.[30]

The traditional view of customers puts them in the position of buying an end product or service. Even in this traditional view, customers can influence product or service characteristics; however, in the closing "value capture" stages, a transaction takes place, and the relationship between the organization and customer ends. In contrast, a contemporary, customer-individualized company is one where value is *created* in partnership with customers. Importantly, value creation is related to the notion of an enduring relationship with customers and creation of value from dynamic, growing markets. The traditional model is fundamentally based on transactions, and capturing value from the fixed pie, where the size of the pie is calculated by static industry market-size analysis.

A company's being customer individualized has obvious implications for all aspects of the organization, but at this point, let's focus on the implications for how the business deals with customers in four particular areas: (1) brands as communities, (2) reduction in marketing costs, (3) customer firing, and (4) fact-based decision making.

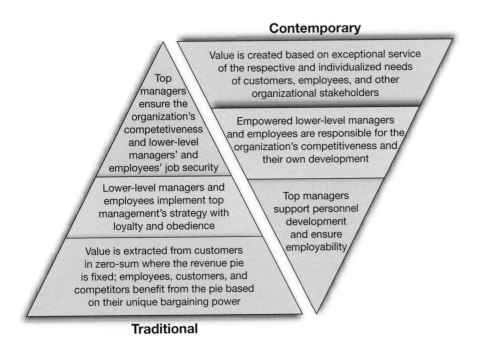

Figure 4 The Customer-Individualized Company

Source: Mason A. Carpenter.

Contemporary

Value is created based on exceptional service of the respective and individualized needs of customers, employees, and other organizational stakeholders

Top managers ensure the organization's competetiveness and lower-level managers' and employees' job security

Empowered lower-level managers and employees are responsible for the organization's competitiveness and their own development

Lower-level managers and employees implement top management's strategy with loyalty and obedience

Top managers support personnel development and ensure employability

Value is extracted from customers in zero-sum where the revenue pie is fixed; employees, customers, and competitors benefit from the pie based on their unique bargaining power

Traditional

BRANDS AS COMMUNITIES

Brands and branding seem more important in attracting and retaining customers than ever before. A *brand* is intangible; it is a collection of perceptions that exists in the mind of the consumer. Based on this definition, *branding* is a set of activities that introduce, develop, and reinforce the collection of customer perceptions. Such definitions suggest that brands are built through a combination of communications and experiences, which has led some to suggest that a brand is more analogous to the notion of a community than it is to any more tangible notion of a product or service.

Specifically, *brand community* is the term social scientists use to describe like-minded consumers who identify with a particular brand and share significant traits, which marketing researchers Albert Muniz and Thomas O'Guinn describe as "shared consciousness, rituals, traditions, and a sense of moral responsibility."[31] The research of Muniz and O'Guinn shows that consumers may organize into these communities to share their experiences of a brand. Conversely, consumers in an identifiable brand community represent a cohesive group that reflects the brand's values.

Companies where the notion of brand community is most keenly seen include Harley-Davidson, Apple Computer, Saab, and Starbucks. While these are high-profile firms, not every company needs to be an Apple or a Harley-Davidson to develop a brand community. For a brand community to exist, the minimum entry criteria appear to be (1) consumers who can be clearly segmented based on the brand (e.g., Harley-Davidson riders) and (2) the existence of mechanisms for consumers to engage in public experience of the brand. With this definition, then, the dedicated consumers of Peet's Coffee and Tea would reasonably be part of a brand community.

The power of the notion of brand communities is twofold. First, because brand community goes beyond the simple definition of a brand, it implies that firms can manage customers' relationships with the brand in the way that service businesses and clubs manage relationships with members. That is, the firm can work on building the relationship with customers by increasing the apparent benefits of membership. Sometimes these benefits make the brand even more "sticky" than one might rationally expect. Sticky brands are those where customers have a hard time disengaging from interaction with the product. For example, urban Harley riders sometimes joke that they can't afford to get rid of their Harley because that would also mean that they would lose all their friends.[32]

The second part of brand-community power is that there is a core group of power users—brand enthusiasts—who actively promote the use and adoption of the brand community's key products or services. Many managers understand that visible consumers of a brand, particularly members of the brand community, become the brand's best promoters. Where marketing and advertising face an increasingly fragmented number of channels and venues, a brand community allows the firm to focus on a core group of enthusiasts and leverage their word-of-mouth promotion with other traditional media.

While there are costs involved with the development and management of brand communities, the benefits of such things as word-of-mouth buzz marketing often outweigh them. Moreover, because the bulk of promotion costs are focused on a discernable core group, marketing and advertising efforts are likely to be much more effective, or at least the results of respective initiatives can be more easily tracked and learned from.

REDUCTION IN MARKETING COSTS

The notion of brand communities gives some managers an opportunity to focus their investments in marketing. However, with most organizations, there tends be a lack of clear understanding of the firm's salient brand communities. For these businesses, the boundaries of its brand communities are rough and unclear.

Regardless of whether the boundaries of the community are understood, tough times tend to promote a willingness among managers to cut costs. While cost cutting may indeed be necessary, the need to cut costs should not be confused with the need to make equal cuts across the board. Across-the-board marketing cuts imply three things. First, they imply that no marketing activity is understood to have a greater impact of firm performance than another activity. If the marketing is tied to specific products or services, then cutting across the board suggests that each product or service is equal in terms of competitive positioning and future prospects. Second, because marketing is treated as containing a homogeneous set of activities and underlying related products or services, this communicates that the firm does not really have a good handle on what leads to what—that is, marketing dollars have been doled out haphazardly, without any clear underlying logic about the return on investment of those marketing dollars. The third implication is that future customer demand is affected only by future advertising dollars and not by investments in marketing made today.

To look at these three implications at work, let's consider a hypothetical scenario in which Microsoft is evaluating whether it should cut back its marketing spending in the last month of 2008. After all, the economy is clearly in a recession and, so the truism goes, companies in recessionary times need to cut costs. Cutting spending across the board will affect Microsoft's software and Xbox games divisions equally. However, given that more Xboxes are sold around December than at any other time of year, such across-the-board cuts would be wrong-headed. Now that we have determined that Microsoft should provide more relative marketing support to Xbox than to software at year-end, we need to decide how that marketing is managed—point of sale, direct paper or e-mail, television, and so on. You get the idea. The better Microsoft's managers have tracked customers' responses to the different marketing media, the better it can understand which levers to pull and, potentially, which levers to pull less or not at all.

The third implication, the relationship between current marketing and future customer behavior, is critical in the hypothetical Microsoft scenario. For well-positioned companies, a recent marketing study showed that an economic recession should not prompt marketing cutbacks but rather an aggressive increase in marketing spending to achieve superior business performance.[33] While somewhat counterintuitive, this conclusion is not new. The first study to substantiate this view was carried out during the U.S. recession of 1923 when advertising executive Roland Vaile monitored 200 companies across America, noting their marketing expenditure and subsequent sales revenue. In April 1927 he reported, in an article he wrote for *Harvard Business Review*, that the companies which advertised the most during that period experienced the largest increases in sales.[34]

More recent research shows that firms entering a recession with a pre-established strategic emphasis on marketing; an entrepreneurial culture; and a sufficient reserve of underutilized workers, cash, and spare production capacity are best positioned to approach recessions as opportunities to strengthen their competitive advantage.[35] "Athletes often choose times of stress to mount attacks: strong runners and bicycle racers may increase their pace on hills or under other challenging conditions. . . . In a similar vein, proactive marketing includes both the sensing of the existence of the opportunity (a tough hill and fatigued opponents) and an aggressive response (possessing the necessary strength or nerve) to the opportunity."[36] In terms of specific examples, the study reminds us of companies that weathered storms and succeeded. These include:

Procter & Gamble—During the Great Depression, P&G pushed Ivory soap.

Intel—During the 1990–1991 economic difficulty, Intel rolled out the campaign "Intel Inside."

Wal-Mart—Wal-Mart launched its "Everyday Low Prices" campaign in 2000–2001.

Conversely, the study finds that firms without these strategic marketing traits are unlikely to derive economic benefits from a proactive marketing response during a recession. Such companies are better served by not increasing marketing spending until conditions improve. "Those firms with a strategic emphasis on marketing have already put in place the programs that help them derive value from their marketing activities (e.g., well-recognized brands, differentiated products, targeted communications, good support and service, etc.)," the authors say. "Thus, Wal-Mart would more likely benefit than the much weaker K-Mart franchise if they had both chosen to increase spending during the most recent recession."[37]

FIRING CUSTOMERS (LESS CAN MEAN MORE)

While it may sound sacrilegious, the notion of firing customers is based on very solid ground and the experience and roots of some of today's best companies. Strategy guru Kim Warren describes it like this:

What is needed [during tough times] is to bring the business back to a good quality "core". In mild cases, this may mean no more than ceasing to serve a small fraction of customers, dropping a few unpopular products and—regrettably—losing just a few of the staff who are no longer needed to support that now-unprofitable business. In more serious cases, it can be necessary to take a knife to the bad-quality periphery of the business. This may mean shutting down whole segments of customers, discontinuing whole classes of products or services, closing down associated capacity and shutting operations in marginal regions. This can be scary. When sales are down because of tough market conditions, it's bold to cut business still further, which is why management is often reluctant and goes for the "cuts across the board" approach. However, pulling back to a healthy core of customers, products, channels, and operating units can substantially improve profits, even while revenues are cut. Much more important, though, is that this change puts the system back to a state where it can develop strongly into the future once again—rather as a gardener prunes weaker branches back so a plant's energy is focused on the stronger limbs, management is pruning the weak activities that are dragging back the whole business so that remaining resources can start working again.[38]

But what does this mean in terms of action? Let's look first at some of the sources of success of Dell Computer, now one of the largest technology companies in the world, and then Best Buy, a top consumer products retailer.

You are likely familiar with Dell today, but the source of Dell's success, including its powerful Dell Direct model, lies in its initial strategy of selling custom-assembled PCs directly to technologically savvy individuals. Why was Dell's initial foray into PCs such an economic and strategic home-run? The beauty of Dell's strategy was that savvy customers knew exactly what they wanted and how PCs worked. Therefore, they could be very specific with their orders and require little to no after-sales service. Also, because the PCs were built to order, Dell did not have to maintain an inventory of finished PCs. Instead, Dell would custom build each unit, based on a customer order, and in cases where a particular part was back-ordered, it could substitute it with a higher-performing part and still make money and ship the computer on time. This custom-manufacturing or assembly approach meant that, unlike retail stores, Dell could maintain modest inventories and almost completely avoid technological obsolescence.

While Dell has had some strategy missteps in recent years, including its sorry efforts to sell flat-screen TVs to home theater enthusiast through its website, the core build-to-order strategy is very solid. Dell has successfully replicated the strategy in the PC-gamer brand Alienware, a high-performance computer game PC maker that Dell acquired in 2006.[39]

Let's look at a second example, featuring electronics retailer Best Buy. In November 2004, *The Wall Street Journal* reported that consumer electronics retailer Best Buy's new customer approach was to shun the "devils" among its customers.[40] This approach, mirroring the guidance of consultants and business authors Larry Selden and Geoff Colvin, followed three principles:[41]

1. Think of a company not as a group of products or services or functions or territories but as a portfolio of customers.

2. Every company's portfolio of customers can and must be managed to produce superior returns for shareowners—meaning a consistently better-than-average share price appreciation—not just to produce earnings per share or EBITDA or revenue growth or customer satisfaction or anything else.

3. Companies enhance customer profitability and drive their stock by creating, communicating, and executing competitively dominant customer value propositions. (Think of this as the complete experience a firm delivers to its customers.)

This approach also parallels and complements the notion of brand communities. Moving on with our example, the "customer centricity" initiative, led by Best Buy's CEO Brad Anderson, was based on an analysis of the purchase histories of several customer groups. The central idea was to revamp stores according to the most lucrative types of customers the stores served—the "angels" among the company's customers. Best Buy's angels are customers who boost profits at the consumer electronics giant by snapping up high-definition televisions, portable electronics, and newly released DVDs without waiting for markdowns or rebates. The devils are its worst customers. They buy products, apply for rebates, return the purchases, and then buy them back at returned-merchandise discounts. They load up on "loss leaders," severely discounted merchandise designed to boost store traffic, and then flip the goods at a profit on eBay. They slap down rock-bottom price quotes from websites and demand that Best Buy make good on its lowest-price pledge. "They can wreak enormous economic havoc," says Anderson.

Both the Dell and Best Buy examples provide a means of thinking about (and even acting on) which customers—in cooperation with the actions of the firm, its managers, and employees—create the most value for all. In many cases, and tough times in particular, an organization that does less (i.e., is more decisive about the customers it caters to) actually creates more (in terms of value).

DATA- AND FACT-BASED CUSTOMER DECISIONS

This section leverages the emerging science of evidence-based management, which is based on the model of evidence-based medicine. Evidence-based medicine, guided by the belief that doctors' actions should be supported by data and facts, dates back some 200 years or more. (You can, for instance, thank evidence-based medicine for the elimination of the practice of bloodletting—that is, draining a portion of your blood for ailments ranging from a cold, to alcoholism, to pneumonia—which, as often as not, created more problems than the ailment it was meant to treat.)

Similarly, evidence-based management emphasizes the imperative to substitute facts for conventional wisdom or management intuition (where intuition can often take the form of pet projects). Using evidence-based management, for example, you would show or predict the relationship between marketing spending and sales before making changes to the marketing budget. The general idea is that, if you do not understand the underlying relationship, then why does it matter that you spend money on marketing (or anything, for that matter) at all? During tough times, understandably, one of the preconceptions is that decreases in advertising spending will not affect future sales. As you saw earlier, however, this is a dangerous half-truth.

Why isn't evidence-based management more widely used? One set of business experts suggests that many managers substitute their own personal theories ("half-truths" or "industry orthodoxies") for facts—sort of like making up the facts to justify an action as you go along.[42] These half-truths are based on some facts, but because they are only partly true, they are also partly false, which provides the early seeds of major problems. Because tough times put managers under pressure, managers may be more likely than usual to take actions based on hunches or focus investments in pet projects. As a result, small mistakes can fester into larger, systematic organizational ailments and diseases.

Success stories about evidence-based decision making provide exemplars such as Harrah's (casinos) and Yahoo! or Google (search engines), settings and firms that collect and catalog large amounts of data. Moreover, both Yahoo! and Google are constantly launching business experiments—that is, trying out new products or services and analyzing the data surrounding the company and customer experience with the product or service. But there are also firms in these industries that collect data but don't bring it into their decision-making processes. So access to data is not really the only barrier to analyzing and acting on data.

Where data are not collected or readily available, there is still opportunity to begin an evidence-based decision-making process. One recent story about evidence-based management chronicles an executive team that was berating its sales and marketing staff for the firm's dismal performance, while sales and marketing were complaining about how hard it was to sell an inferior product. Then the top executives left the office to visit the retail stores where their product was sold and found that salespeople actually tried to talk them out of the purchase; "every executive encountered salespeople who tried to dissuade them from buying the firm's [products], citing the excessive price, weak feature set, clunky appearance, and poor customer service."[43] Thus, the ability to engage in evidence-based management can start with very simple information and low-tech information-gathering approaches. It is valuable to start with an assessment of key business assumptions and identify which of these assumptions are half-truths masquerading for an opportunity to conduct some data gathering and analysis.

WHY NOW?

Tough times provide managers with an opportunity to find out who their customers really are and what bundle of experiences those customers believe they are engaging through the purchase of one or more services or products. Tough times also give managers opportunity and motivation to pare business back to the truly profitable core. As one strategic thinker observes, "really smart management, of course, anticipates the risk of creating this problem in the first place, and avoids it by more thoughtful expansion efforts in the good times."[44] Finally, tough times provide managers a chance to begin experimenting with evidence-based management. Under pressure, individuals tend to fall back on routines and behaviors that are based on preconceptions and assumptions. If these routines and behaviors are faulty (and many have been proven to be so), then management is building a very shaky foundation on which to erect the future firm.

Human Capital

You have certainly heard or read the familiar declaration "our employees are our most important asset." While many managers would agree with the spirit of that statement, very few can tell you why that is true or should be true. Moreover, among the wealth of assets that an organization can tap into, human capital is one of the most complex (next to social capital). *Human capital* is the set of skills that an employee acquires on the job, through training, and through experience and that increase an employee's value to the firm and in the marketplace.

Beyond notations for salaries, bonuses, health care, and pensions, human capital does not appear on balance sheets or income statements. This further contributes to the perception of many that areas such as strategic human resource management are soft and fuzzy. And while human capital may not exist on a company's books, it is a notoriously popular area for making cuts in tough times. Therefore, let's take a look at approaches to managing human capital in tough times, as well as alternatives to across-the-board cuts (another favorite management tool in tough times).

MANAGING HUMAN CAPITAL THROUGH TOUGH TIMES

Because downsizing is a popular management tool to use during tough times, let's look at it first. It is widely understood today that downsizing has a positive effect on short-term cost reduction objectives but a negative effect on innovation, competitiveness, and longer-term profitability.[45] Beyond the view of downsizing as a *blunt sword*, we also know that managers should consider the different ways that downsizing can be achieved. The advantages and disadvantages of several approaches are summarized in Figure 5.

As you can see, each of these alternatives has benefits and costs. The body of knowledge on downsizing suggests that organizations can minimize (but not eliminate) costs when they have a clear strategy and choose the downsizing approach that is appropriate for that strategy.

ALTERNATIVES TO DOWNSIZING

There are a number of viable alternatives to downsizing and even, counterintuitively, the tactic of hiring when the rest of the world is cutting back. Let's take a look at five ways that human capital can be preserved through tough times.

Change the Form of Compensation
The first way to preserve human capital in tough times is through the compensation system, following the lead of many Japanese companies. If annual pay is based on something like 70 to 80 percent salary, and the balance is based on firm performance, then when the business is unprofitable, it is essentially lowering what it pays out in salaries. A variation on this scenario is the piece-rate system employed by companies such as Lincoln Electric. This approach rewards individuals based on their productivity and will naturally adjust payout with changes in the health of the economy. The key risk accompanying this approach is that competitors can hire workers

Approach	Advantages	Disadvantages
Across the board cuts.	Easy for managers to understand, communicate, and apply; pain is shared across the organization	Not strategic, in the sense than no individual is deemed more important to the future of the firm than another; efficient parts of the business are hurt more than the inefficient ones; little or no opportunity to upgrade skills by moving better employees to other areas in the firm.
Make cuts to non-core areas and outsource or eliminate them.	Higher-cost labor is replaced with outsourced labor; immediate cost savings.	Mistakes made in classifying core versus non-core parts of the firm; potential longer-term cost increases and quality control problems associated with outsourced functions; costs and capabilities needed to coordinate subcontractors; lack of control over subcontractors.
Removing a level of the organization.	Decision making can become more decentralized; cuts are spread across the organization.	Loss of organizational memory; senior managers can become overburdened; possible high retraining and transitions costs.
Drop product or service lines.	Can be more tightly linked to the organization's strategy; concentrates downsizing to one or a few business units.	Shifts burden to a few people; unanticipated losses of business in the core based on elimination of 'peripheral' businesses.
Early retirement	Downsizing focuses on those able and willing to leave; higher paid people tend to be those most likely to leave (though this can be offset by retirement or severance package costs).	Not strategic; the first to leave will be the most able; loss of organizational memory and tacit capabilities can be severe.

Figure 5 Alternative Means of Downsizing

Source: Mason A. Carpenter.

away by eliminating the performance-based criterion. Similarly, the program becomes ineffective when bonuses are paid out even when performance is poor.

Cut Pay, Not People, Across the Board The second alternative builds on an implication of a performance-based pay system. Specifically, across-the-board cuts are made not in terms of downsizing employees but instead to the levels of pay for all employees. Cuts can be based on a percentage by level or some other formula to help adjust for the fact that small changes in pay for lower-paid employees have a greater negative marginal effect on their welfare than similar dollar changes in higher-paid people. The key premise is that all employees (including managers) share in the pain but benefit from still having jobs. A variation on this across-the-board-cuts approach is the reduction of employment hours, in conjunction with pay cuts, during slower times of the year. This has been a long-standing practice at Hewlett-Packard, for instance; the company essentially shut its doors for several weeks at the end of 2008. Like the first approach, the major drawback here is that the firm is temporarily uncompetitive in the labor market.

Encourage Part-time Work Firms that follow this second approach to downsizing are sometimes surprised to find that not all their employees want to return to full-time work. This leads to the third alternative to downsizing, which is the active use of part-time workers and the encouragement of leaves of absences and sabbaticals. This partially accounts for the growing category of temporary workers at all levels. In some organizations, such an approach is called "flex-time" or "time-banking." The flex-time alternative to downsizing can be executed in a variety of ways. For example, when automaker BMW asks employees to work overtime when demand is high (in the good times), instead of receiving overtime pay, employees can bank those hours. When BMW has to go to shorter shifts or shorter work weeks (during the tough times), employees can then draw on their banked hours and receive full pay for part-time work.

Redesign the Work The fourth approach involves the redesign of work within a firm. This alternative to downsizing can take a number of forms. Sometimes it can be managed piecemeal. For instance, a company may eliminate the use of PowerPoint presentations in any meeting. From the boardroom to sales meetings, managers are amazed at how much time is freed up when their employees are spending time with customers and executing the strategy instead of agonizing over the colors and graphics on slides and the ordering of slides. Firms are also finding that this is a very effective way to cut down on their consulting bills.

Consider Cisco Systems's approach to downsizing during the first recession of this century. In 2001, as deteriorating financial performance forced the elimination of 8,500 jobs, Cisco redesigned roles and responsibilities to improve cross-functional alignment and reduce duplication.[46] The more collaborative environment fostered by these moves increased workplace satisfaction and productivity for many employees. Initiatives like Cisco's succeed when companies focus on redesigning jobs and retaining talent at the outset of downsizing efforts.

Other examples of systematic work redesign include the gradual implementation of lean processes in manufacturing as well as service areas (called "lean in the office"). Lean is a generic process management philosophy derived mostly from the Toyota Production System but also from other sources. It is renowned for its focus on reduction of Toyota's original "seven wastes" in order to improve overall customer value.[47] Lean is often linked with Six Sigma because of that methodology's emphasis on reduction of process variation (or increases in its converse, smoothness). Toyota's steady growth from a small player to the most valuable and biggest car company in the world has brought attention to how it has achieved this, making lean a hot topic in management science in the first decade of the twenty-first century. Essentially, lean processes allow a firm to create more value with less capital (human, financial, and physical). In the best of lean implementation cases, organizations use organic attrition to reduce their labor force, or, through improvement in quality and customer engagement, grow the business to meet the human capital levels already in the firm.

Hire, Don't Fire The fifth and final alternative is to be a contrarian. That is, while others are cutting their employees loose, you are recruiting the best and brightest of the newly freed-up human capital. This approach presents two key benefits. First, job candidate quality tends to be higher when other firms are downsizing and jobs are hard to find. Second, the organization is better positioned to exploit the eventual economic upturn. This latter advantage also suggests that new hires be made based on the needs of the future firm, not just to fill a gap related to how the organization has operated in the past. For instance, in addition to finding employees with needed technical or professional skills, organizations can bring in people who have worked with or implemented lean systems, balanced scorecards, or fact-based customer decision making.

WHAT TO DO WITH THE "KEEPERS"?

Managers spend a great deal of time determining who should stay and who should go as part of their efforts to control human capital costs during tough times. However, they tend to give little thought or attention to what should be done to develop those who get to stay—the "keepers." Tough times present a good opportunity to develop employee skill sets and build up the caliber of human capital through internal and external training. In addition to increasing employee productivity and effectiveness, such actions can increase loyalty and decrease the risk that anxious employees might jump ship. Beyond employee development, tough economic conditions also provide time for planning, networking with customers, and analysis. If sales are slow, why not invest those hours in serving the needs of the business by developing better insights into the drivers of customer needs; creating a shared understanding of the mission, vision, and strategy; and building models that help the firm understand relationships between the underlying drivers of performance and actual performance (see the earlier section on fact- and data-based customer decision making).

WHY NOW?

Tough times make everyone anxious, and there is a tendency for individuals to seek change to show, to themselves and others, that they are in some sort of control over the situation. "When times are tough, the tough get going." Unfortunately, in many firms, the choice to stay or go is being made by someone else. Just as problematic is the possibility that the organization's best managers and employees can be among the first to leave because they will have the most choices in the field of alternative employers (even the alternative of starting up their own business, as a competitor, or in a new industry). As you reconnect with the business's customer core, you can better identify the aspects of human capital that are critical to serving this core well. Because tough times also can leave employees with extra time on their hands, why not exploit the situation to engage them more fully with customers, strategy, and the data needed to understand the relationship among strategy, customers, and performance?

Social Networks and Social Capital

Why do employers ask for a resume as a precursor to a job interview? Part of the reason is that they want to see what you have *done*. But why is this information important? It is important because employers hope that it will also help them understand what you can *do*. However, we are learning that much of what an individual (and an organization, for that matter) can do is based on his or her social capital.

Your *social network* is the structure of personal and professional relationships you have with others. *Social capital*, in turn, is the resources—such as ideas, information, money, and trust—available in and through personal and business social networks. *Networking* and a social network are related, but they are very different in important ways. Networking is what you do to create your social network, but some of it will naturally be a function of your friends, family, and work environment (e.g., your boss, colleagues, customers, and simply where your office is located). Importantly, networking may connect you to other people, but those other people can potentially connect you to many, many more people. Even if you do not like the stigma associated with networking, it is critical to understand the consequences (in terms of constraint and opportunities) of your social network's structure. Finally, you can have social capital, as can organizations. However, because social capital is based on relationships, no single person can claim ownership, but it is nonetheless important and manageable.

There are three key reasons why social capital is important for effective management in general; these three reasons are particularly important for managing effectively in tough times. Social capital tells us how work gets done in an organization; it is the consequence of social networking, which in turn is the structure behind the formal organizational chart; finally, social capital is an essential ingredient in innovation. Let's look at each of these in turn.

SOCIAL CAPITAL AS A VEHICLE FOR GETTING THINGS DONE

To understand the importance of social capital for getting things done, let's explore the well-known and lesser-known stories of Paul Revere. For most American schoolchildren, this story has practically become legend. Specifically, Paul Revere rode from Boston one early morning in April 1775 to warn the surrounding communities that the British were on their way. By the time the British had begun their march toward Lexington, on the following day, the colonial resistance was already well organized and in place. As a result, the British were soundly beaten at Concord, giving rise to what history would later record as the American Revolution.

While the result of Paul Revere's ride may be history, let's look a little closer at the sequence of events:

> On the night of 17 April 1775, two men rode different routes from outside Boston to Lexington warning communities along the way of the imminent threat from the British army. The message delivered by Paul Revere and William Dawes on their midnight rides was dramatic: the next day would see the British army marching on Lexington to arrest colonial leaders and then on to Concord to seize colonial guns and ammunition. Both Revere and Dawes carried the identical message through just as many towns over just as many miles. Paul Revere's message spread like wildfire in communities such as Charlestown and Medford, but Dawes' message failed to catch fire, with the result that in towns such as Waltham even the local militia leaders weren't aware of the British moves. Why was there a difference in the reception of this identical message? Evidence suggests that Paul Revere was connected to an extensive network of strategic relationships whereas William Dawes' connections were less useful. Paul Revere "knew everybody. . . . When he came upon a town, he would have known exactly whose door to knock on, who the local militia leader was, who the key players in town were" (Gladwell, 2000: 23). Not only did Revere alert whole towns to the looming threat, the leaders in these towns themselves sent riders to alert the surrounding areas. Dawes' message failed to spread through the network whereas Revere's message rapidly diffused.[48]

This simple story of Paul Revere's ride provides a salient example of the importance of social capital for getting things done. Paul Revere had a lot more social capital than did Dawes, and as a result can take much of the credit for frustrating the attack of the British. Social capital is a function of network size, and in that sense, it looks as though Dawes and Revere had similar networks, in terms of the number of towns visited. However, while Dawes and Revere had networks of the same size, the individuals Dawes contacted did not have their own larger social networks. That is, Revere had access to a much broader group of people because his direct ties were with individuals we might call "super connectors." Indeed, in a number of social networks—be they university settings or big businesses—you will find that a small number of people provide a disproportionate number of contacts to others, albeit indirectly. Finally, Revere's direct contacts in each city were also diverse, in that they tapped into networks that were not only broad but different, too. As a result, Revere was able to spread his news like wildfire, while Dawes was not.

This anecdote about Paul Revere has at least two implications for getting things done during tough times. First, having an understanding of the organization's social network will help managers get their work done more quickly and more effectively during tough times. Managers' social capital is enriched when they cultivate relationships with the super connectors, and many super connectors are not in formal positions of authority or power. (Although their network position gives them power, it is up to them how they use it.) Second, because social networks are so important to getting things done, the elimination of one person from the organization could create a much larger unforeseen disruption, with the financial damage outweighing any benefit from a reduction in payroll. Social capital typically does not appear on one's resume. Put another way, during tough times, the battle is on, and you probably don't want to fire your organization's next Paul Revere.

SOCIAL NETWORKS AS INVISIBLE STRUCTURE

If social networks are the vehicle by which work gets done, then you should not be surprised to learn that social networks are the invisible structure in the organization—the structure that fosters or frustrates good performance and strategic change. Organizations that understand and actively manage their internal social networks—and even those networks that span the organization and suppliers, customers, and other stakeholders—are more likely to benefit from the social capital such networks create. At the very least, managers may be more cognizant of how different members of the network contribute to the flow of resources in and out of the network—whether those resources are information, knowledge, new ideas, or money.

Recently, social network experts Rob Cross, Stephen Borghatti, and Andrew Parker have categorized five types of internal social networks, with the aim of providing a way to think about and manage the influence of such networks on social capital and, ultimately, firm performance.[49] Based on an employee questionnaire, a network map is created around the focal process of interest (communication, information, and so on). For example, communication networks are important in the sense that they reflect regular interaction among individuals regarding specific issues or in general. Understanding communication network structure can help you identify communication bottlenecks or isolated employees. An information network reflects who goes to whom to get facts and figures. Whereas a communication network looks at the broader level of dialogue, an information network shows the flow of information that affects how (and how well) individual work and team work is getting done. For example, as shown in Figure 6, the map of an information network can show how information flows, and help identify missed opportunities or communication gaps.[50] For instance, based on the map, Janet is a super connector with 6 direct links to other people. Cindi has only 3 connections, but holds a powerful position as the sole *boundary spanner* between different groups. Jeff and Judy have the shortest paths to all others; they have an excellent view of what's going on. Finally, Cho is isolated from all but Rob.

The third type of network is a project network, or problem-solving network. This type of network is related to efforts to solve particular problems or complete a defined project. Human nature suggests that individuals seek out information and relationships from and with individuals who are most like them. Unfortunately, a problem-solving network can

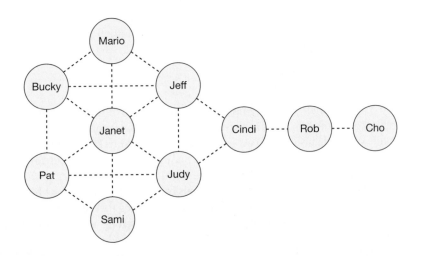

Figure 6 A Network Map Based on Information Flows

Source: Mason A. Carpenter.

therefore tend to be clique-like or narrow. Also, "strong problem solving networks often ensure that people are solving the right problem, thus improving individual and network performance."[51] Increasingly, problem-solving groups, particular project-based ones, include external consultants and temporary workers. One large insurance company, facing pressure because of tough times, sought first to control costs by making across-the-board cuts to its consulting and temporary workforce. Unfortunately, a key project on which the firm's strategy depended was being led by two of those consultants. Oops!

SOCIAL CAPITAL AS A VEHICLE FOR INNOVATION

Social capital and social networks are essential ingredients in the ability of firms to generate new ideas—whether innovations in products or services or in improving how the organization gets work done. As a recent *McKinsey Quarterly* article notes:

> Chances are your organization has some people who are passionate about innovation and others who feel uncomfortable about any topic related to change. Recent academic research finds that differences in individual creativity and intelligence matter far less for innovation than connections and networks—for example, networked employees can realize their innovations and make them catch on more quickly. Since new ideas seem to spur more new ideas, networks generate a cycle of innovation. Furthermore, effective networks allow people with different kinds of knowledge and ways of tackling problems to cross-fertilize ideas. By focusing on getting the most from innovation networks, leaders can therefore capture more value from existing resources, without launching a large-scale change-management program.[52]

The authors of this article drew some of their conclusions from recent research by Lee Fleming and Matt Marx.[53] Fleming and Marx contrast the historically disconnected world of scientists and engineers with the current and emerging clusters of social-network-based innovation. One of their startling observations is that a disproportionate number of inventors account for most of the new innovation breakthroughs. Moreover, and building on the notion of super connectors introduced earlier in this section, they label these key inventors *gatekeepers*. These gatekeepers operate across organizations in a way that connects other large but previously disconnected social networks.

This understanding of how social networks relate to innovation also resonates with social network research which finds that, even beyond the discovery of good ideas, individuals who connect otherwise disconnected individuals and groups are more likely to be paid more, have better performance evaluations, and be more likely to be promoted.[54] In conclusion, Fleming and Marx argue that "managerial attention should focus on identifying, retaining, and enabling *gatekeepers*—technical professionals who span organizational boundaries, accelerating the process of invention by contributing to and capitalizing on interfirm spillovers of technical knowledge."[55]

WHY NOW?

While much managerial attention is paid to the characteristics of individuals in a firm and the structure of relationships summarized in an organizational chart, these pieces of the puzzle provide very little insight into how work actually gets done. In good times and tough times, the invisible structure provided by social networks can foster or frustrate progress and success. Because tough times provide little cushion for errors, making uninformed changes to staffing that disrupt the otherwise invisible flow of resources can have significant unintended negative consequences. Conversely, changes that leverage and enhance the power of the organization's social capital create for it a strong and enduring bridge to better times.

Innovation and Change

Management guru Peter Drucker once observed that "business has only two functions—marketing and innovation." (He went on to cynically note that all other business functions are expenses.)[56] While the current recession might suggest that other functions, such as finance, operations, and so on, might be important, too, the notion that innovation is a key source of competitive advantage has some fairly strong anecdotal support. For example, leading innovators such as Apple, Disney, and Research in Motion (maker of the BlackBerry wireless handheld devices), are experiencing strong revenues in areas where they have exciting products and services; even otherwise downtrodden stock analysts are asking whether such "creatives" are perhaps recession resistant.

However, knowing that innovation is important is a far cry from having the ability to create an innovative organization. As one set of experts has observed:

> Like short skirts, innovation has traditionally swung into and out of fashion: popular in good times and tossed back into the closet in downturns. But as globalization tears down the geographic boundaries and market barriers that once kept businesses from achieving their potential, a company's ability to innovate—to tap the fresh value-creating ideas of its employees and those of its partners, customers, suppliers, and other parties beyond its own boundaries—is anything but faddish. In fact, innovation has become a core driver of growth, performance, and valuation.[57]

WHAT DOES INNOVATION LOOK LIKE?

While we like to think of innovations as products or services that are entirely new to the planet, experience has shown that timing plays a big role in the success of innovations. For example, very few of us remember Apple's Newton handheld computer, which was a dismal failure. However, just some 10 years later, a similar product—the PalmPilot—seemed to create an industry all by itself.

What do great innovations have in common? Innovations, and the new markets that often accompany them, seem to have five common characteristics: (1) something is reduced, (2) something is eliminated, (3) something is created, (4) something is raised, and (5) something stays the same. These new market creation factors are shown in Figure 7.

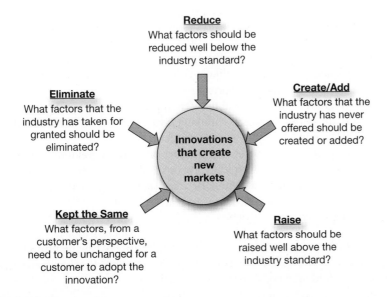

Figure 7 Innovations That Create New Markets

Source: Mason A. Carpenter.

The first four characteristics are summarized in the Blue Ocean Strategy framework popularized by strategy researchers Chan Kim and Renee Mauborgne.[58] The fifth characteristic was developed through the work of their colleagues, Mason Carpenter and W. Gerry Sanders, authors of the best-selling textbook *Strategic Management: A Dynamic Perspective.*[59] The general idea behind the first four changes is that an innovation will offer something new, but not necessarily because it is simply adding more features or costs. For instance, Amazon.com became successful because it provided a greater selection of books than any other store on the planet (increase), allowed greater convenience when shopping for books (reduced time needed), developed a logistics and software infrastructure to manage the process (create/add), and threatened to make brick-and-mortar stores obsolete (eliminate).

New markets can be created when innovations orchestrate these four characteristics alone. However, experience has shown that the more that customers need to change their behaviors, the more slowly they will adopt an innovation. For this reason, the fifth characteristic—what stays the same—becomes a differentiating factor between innovations that take hold and those that do not or do so only slowly. For instance, e-books have not really taken off, even though there are increasing numbers of ways for them to be purchased and read. Similarly, innovations such as digital video recorders (e.g., TiVo) have been slow to gain users because consumers have to change their behaviors; Skype faces similar obstacles (even though making calls with Skype is free, you often have to call through a PC and also pay for high-speed cable connections). In contrast, Amazon's strategy worked largely because the book—the basic product—remained unchanged (and has been unchanged for the past 600 years), which means that consumers are likely to be uncomfortable abandoning that medium very quickly. Google was a great success as well because it let us use the same browser we were used to but offered a far superior search experience.

HOW INNOVATIVE ARE YOU NOW?

A short survey can help you determine how innovative a company is now. The first part asks whether the firm has innovation processes in place and provides an example of one—the stage-gate process. The second part poses a series of questions about how an innovation might survive an organization's internal climate.

Do You Have a Process for Innovation?

Innovation is just a matter of spending time dreaming up new ideas, right? While giving employees free time to develop product ideas is a good start (as 3M and Google do by allowing employees to spend 10 percent of their time experimenting with new products and services), it is only a start.

Increasingly, experts suggest that the most innovative companies will take the principles and reasoned risk taking of venture capital, private equity, and R&D and bring those perspectives inside the firm to create new products, services, and businesses.[60] One of the key benefits to this migration from external to internal practices is that risk taking becomes a managed process; the notion of project chunking is very relevant here and takes the form of what the best R&D companies call a *stage-gate* process.

The stage-gate process is a type of new product or service development that separates the innovation process into stages (typically five or six of them), with each stage containing a set of parallel, cross-functional activities. Between stages are gates that open or close the door for projects to move to the next stage. Gates act as quality check points in the process. Moreover, gates have a common format:

- **Deliverables.** These are the inputs into the gate review—what the project leader and team propose to deliver. They are the results of the actions of the previous stage and are based on a standard menu of deliverables for each stage.

- **Criteria.** These are questions or metrics on which a project is judged in order to make go/kill and prioritization decisions.

- **Outputs.** These are the results of the gate review—decisions (go/kill/hold/recycle). An action plan is approved, and the date and deliverables for the next gate are agreed on.

A Simple Test Whether or not a firm has some type of innovation process in place, it still may have internal roadblocks to innovation. Managers need to identify the number of new products or services that have been introduced this year. If the answer is none, then that is a pretty good clue about the firm's level of innovation. Even if the answer is something more than none, it is a good exercise to identify the percentage of revenues that come from new products or services.

Companies that aspire to be innovative often set clear and specific new product or service innovation targets. For example, 3M states that 30 percent of sales must come from products that are less than four years old. Similarly, the Gillette subsidiary of P&G states that 40 percent of sales every five years must come from entirely new products.[61]

It is one thing to set such goals and another to achieve them. For innovation goals to be realized, there must be some pathway in the organization for developing new ideas and moving them forward—even if it is just to the beginning of the stage-gate or similar process. Gary Hamel, a business futurist and strategy guru, suggests that firms take this simple four-item test, based on responses from first-level employees, to see whether they can walk the talk in terms of innovation capability:[62]

1. How have you been trained as a business innovator? What investment has the company made in teaching you how to innovate?

2. If you have a new idea, how much bureaucracy do you have to go through to get a small increment of experimental capital? How long is it going to take you to get 20 percent of your time and $5,000 to test your idea? Is that a matter of months, or is it very easy for that to happen?

3. Are you actually being measured on your innovation performance or your team's innovation? Does it influence your compensation?

4. As you look at the management processes in your company, do they tend to help you work as an innovator or get in the way?

Hamel concludes this questioning by observing that the answers will tell management very quickly how big the gap is between a vision that preaches innovation and the actual achievement of it. The questions themselves also provide a pathway for beginning to develop a culture that understands how innovation comes about.

WHY NOW?

Innovation challenges managers and employees to think about solving internal and customer problems in new and exciting ways. Tough times requires that firms both do things better and do different things; this is essentially the definition of innovation. Tough times can become the mother of invention. As Hamel notes,

> To become inspired management innovators, today's executives must learn how to think explicitly about the management orthodoxies that bound their thinking—the habits, dogmas, and conceits they've never taken the trouble to challenge. For example, many people believe that it takes a crisis to change a large organization, and when we look at the evidence this seems to be the case.[63]

Moreover, an innovative organization is one that is more likely to attract and retain the human capital that takes it farther when times are good. Thus, the capacity to innovate and accumulate the best human and social capital become self-reinforcing.

Financial Capital

Financial capital, in the form of cash flow and financial health, is essential to the operation of any and every organization. Indeed, even not-for-profits such as churches, schools, and governments have bills to pay. Without good financial health, good intentions do not allow a business to invest in other benefits to society, such as social and environmental activities. However, in order to understand the determinants and levers related to financial help, you need a better picture of what leads to those numbers. This is where a balanced scorecard comes in.

USING THE BALANCED SCORECARD TO UNDERSTAND FINANCIAL HEALTH

You have probably already learned a bit about balanced scorecards from other sources. The balanced scorecard concept, created by David Norton and Robert Kaplan, is an outgrowth of the so-called value-based management techniques that first appeared in the late 1980s.[64] Scorecards help highlight cause-and-effect relationships among performance drivers and identify the links to strategic outcomes. But a balanced scorecard is not strategic planning, Norton insists. "It's a tool that forces you to articulate your strategy. You should be able to look at your scorecard and reverse engineer it to see what the underlying strategy is."[65]

The balanced scorecard was originally introduced to integrate financial and nonfinancial controls in a way that provides a balanced understanding of the determinants of firm performance. It has since evolved into a strategic performance management tool of sorts because it helps managers identify and understand the way that operating controls are tied to strategic controls and, ultimately, firm performance. In this broader sense, a balanced scorecard is a control system that translates an organization's mission, vision, and strategy into specific, quantifiable goals and helps monitor the organization's performance in terms of achieving these goals. This set of relationships is summarized in Figure 8.

You are already familiar with the roles of mission, vision, and strategy. This section focuses on the scorecard, strategy mapping, and how the system brings these together with

Figure 8   The Balanced Scorecard Hierarchy

Source: Mason A. Carpenter.

underlying development projects, including your own personal development. A typical scorecard considers performance in four areas: (1) *financial* (the most traditionally used performance indicator, which includes assessments of measures such as operating costs and return on investment); (2) *customer* (looks at customer satisfaction and retention); (3) *internal* (looks at production and innovation, measuring performance in terms of maximizing profit from current products and following indicators for future productivity); and (4) *learning and growth* (explores the effectiveness of management in terms of measures of employee satisfaction and retention and information system performance).[66]

Importantly, managers should identify the key performance indicators (KPIs) that they will use to gauge an organization's health in each area. Whether financial or nonfinancial, "the best set of KPIs should be viewed as a forward-looking system of measurements that help managers predict the company's economic performance and spot the need for changes in operations."[67] In choosing KPIs, it is important to remember the adage "what gets measured is what gets done."

THE STRATEGY MAP AS A COMPLEMENT TO THE SCORECARD

Whereas the scorecard identifies financial and nonfinancial areas of performance, the second step in the scorecard process is the development of a strategy map. The idea here is to identify key performance areas in learning and growth and show how they cascade forward into the internal, customer, and financial performance areas. Typically, this is an iterative process in which managers test relationships between the different areas of performance. Your familiarity with evidence-based management will help you with these aspects of the strategy map. In an organization that is a for-profit business, such as IBM, managers would want to be able to show how and why the choice made in each area will ultimately lead to high profitability and stock prices. In contrast, a not-for-profit organization will want to show how investments and spending in each area maximize key stakeholder benefits.

With the scorecard and strategy map in hand, managers break down broad goals into vision strategies for each of the four areas, strategic initiatives, and metrics. Your familiarity with the importance of projects and the notion of chunking (introduced earlier) will be helpful here.

As an example of how the methodology might work, an organization might include in its mission and vision statement a goal of maintaining employee satisfaction. This would likely be the organization's vision in the domain of learning and growth because employee satisfaction is indirectly related to financial performance. Strategies for achieving that learning and growth vision might include approaches such as increasing employee–management communication. Initiatives undertaken to implement the strategy could include, for example, regularly scheduled meetings with employees. Metrics (KPIs) could include quantifications of employee suggestions or employee surveys. Finally, managers would want to test their assumptions about the relationship between employee satisfaction and downstream areas such as internal, customer, and financial performance. For example, satisfied employees may be more productive and less likely to quit (internal), which leads to better products or services and customer relations (customer), which leads to lower employee recruiting and training costs and greater sales and repeat sales (financial). The map should thus reveal the implicit sequence of causal relationships underlying the firm's strategy and resource allocation decisions.

WHY NOW?

The balanced scorecard and its complement, the strategy map, are valuable management tools in good times. They help managers create a balance between short-term needs (productivity) and long-term needs (growth). This is one of the reasons it is called a balanced scorecard. However, in tough times balanced scorecards and strategy maps might be considered essential tools because they help managers understand the ways that changes in one area affect another, including cash flow and bottom-line financial performance. While many managers, when faced with recessionary conditions, want to make changes to their KPIs, from a balanced scorecard perspective, this is putting the cart before the horse. The first question that tough times prompt relates to strategy: Is my strategy still sound? If the strategy changes, then it is appropriate to revisit the entire map, including the KPIs. The caveat here is that you need to be sure you are using the right measure for KPIs. For example, the managers of one business with thousands of retail stores were convinced that voluntary turnover was a key (negative) driver of performance. However, analysis of the data revealed that it really was the turnover of store managers that had the greatest negative impact (and retention of store managers a positive one). With this new degree of understanding, the business was able to focus on the performance driver that mattered most.[68]

Values-Based Leadership

This eighth and final area of activity is brief, not because it is less important than the other seven areas—far from it—but instead because the message here can be stated clearly and concisely. The concept of values-based leadership in a business environment is not just public relations mumbo-jumbo; values-based leadership fosters a willingness among employees to embrace change and help the organization adapt during tough and good times. Moreover, it positively affects the bottom line.

Values-based leadership is the action of articulating the wants and needs of employees by helping them understand and act on the company's shared vision. A values-based leader, as suggested in the upper levels of Richard Barrett's model of values-based leadership shown in Figure 9, inspires employees by listening and understanding their needs and influencing them to make the necessary changes to accomplish the company's shared vision.

How do we know that values-based leadership matters and makes a difference in organizational performance? If you look at all the companies surveyed for such best-selling business books as *Good to Great* and *Built to Last*, you will find that one common factor shared by all great companies is the presence of leaders who visibly and ceaselessly practice values-based leadership. Beyond the concise definition offered earlier, it is helpful to consider the inputs into values-based leadership. Specifically, what would values-based leadership look like if we saw it or experienced it? To answer this question, let's look to one of the world's leading consultants

Figure 9 Barrett's Seven Levels of Values-Based Leadership

Source: Mason A. Carpenter.

on the topics of values-based leadership and cultural transformation, Richard Barrett. Barrett outlines seven levels of actions based on the work of Maslow, that executives, managers, and employees exhibit to build a truly values-driven organization:[69]

Level 1 deals with issues regarding survival and safety. This is the level of the crisis director/accountant. The values we see leaders display at this level of consciousness are profit, financial stability, self-discipline, and employee safety.

Level 2 addresses issues regarding relationships and communication. This is the level of the relationship manager/communicator. The values leaders at this level exhibit are conflict resolution, employee recognition, customer satisfaction, and open communication.

Level 3 speaks to issues regarding performance and best practice. This is the level of the manager/organizer. Typical values at this level of consciousness are results orientation, efficiency, productivity, and quality.

Level 4 deals with issues regarding adaptability and employee participation in decision making. This is the level of the facilitator/influencer. The values we see leaders display at this level of consciousness are courage, innovation, teamwork, and accountability.

Level 5 involves shared values and shared vision. This is the level of the integrator/inspirer. The values displayed at this level of consciousness are enthusiasm, fairness, trust, and integrity.

Level 6 addresses issues regarding community involvement and strategic alliances. This is the level of the mentor/partner. The values shown at this level of consciousness are environmental stewardship, customer collaboration, employee fulfillment, and mentoring.

Level 7 deals with issues regarding ethics and social responsibility. This is the level of the wisdom/visionary. The values we see leaders displaying at this level are compassion, forgiveness, humility, and ease with uncertainty.[70]

WHY NOW?

Companies that are already great have managers throughout the organization who understand and practice values-based leadership. Barrett argues that beliefs are an imperfect decision-making tool and that, given the chaos and complexity of today's tough times, values provide the most flexible mode of decision making. Values-based leadership asks that you anticipate how you come across and empathize with the person on the other side of the table—to put yourself in another person's shoes. The ability to do this comes from being a good listener and conveying a sense of trustworthiness. Tough economic conditions also threaten personal loyalties at a time when such social capital is perhaps most needed. Values-based leadership creates loyalty by managing others in the same way you would want to be managed. If you have a dictatorial style and you discourage independent thinking, then you need to realize that the success of your endeavor will be greatly dependent on your all-individual capabilities; that is, your social network might consist of you alone. Finally, a benefit to being a values-based leader is that others will want to follow you when making career moves. This is often inevitable during tough times. Many successful entrepreneurs have this sort of leadership quality and are followed by former teammates as they go from venture to venture.[71]

What Next?

This supplement has laid out an orderly way of thinking about managing effectively through tough times. On the one hand, many of the observations are supported by evidence of success in a number of businesses around the world. During good times, these are practices that most firms would want to emulate. Indeed, many managers will read each section and say to themselves "I already knew that!" On the other hand, given the anxiety and uncertainty created by tough times, and based on what you see many managers actually doing, what should be *known* and *common sense* seems to be forgotten.

Organization researchers Jeff Pfeffer and Robert Sutton have described this frustrating and perplexing problem as the "knowing–doing gap." They ask, "why is that so many managers know so much about organizational performance, say so many smart things about how to achieve performance, and work so hard, yet are trapped in firms that do so many things they know will undermine performance?"[72] While Pfeffer and Sutton document the knowing–doing gap across many industries and across many different sets of economic conditions, it is during tough times that such gaps will arguably grow and actually become canyons or bottomless pits.

This supplement has sought to remind managers (and students) about what they already know and encourage them to take particular and determined care in applying these known managerial smarts in tough times. Pfeffer and Sutton, in the conclusion of their book, offer a general set of steps that are just as relevant in the context of this supplement and tough times as they are in general for managers seeking to close the knowing–doing gap during good times. Let's look at their eight guidelines, "translated" and adapted into the context of managing during tough times:

Guideline 1: Have a purpose.   Purpose provides individuals with hope and direction. Your purpose expresses your core values—those values exhibited through the mission and vision of the organization and through those exhibited in all the levels of values-based leadership.

Guideline 2: Doing and teaching leads to knowing.   Mission, vision, and strategy are beneficial only to the extent that they foster responsible action. The future is uncertain, but the purpose need not be. Action helps create knowledge where there once was uncertainty; similarly, teaching leads to experimentation, action, and more knowledge.

Guideline 3: Remember Peters' and Waterman's "ready, fire, aim."[73] While many of the companies from *In Search of Excellence* are long gone, one of the key lessons about learning by doing remains more relevant today, during tough times, than ever before. Moreover, acting in the face of uncertainty has the added benefit of providing information for future action versus the undesirable alternative of planning based on intuition, hunches, and habit.

Guideline 4: An absence of risk-taking and mistakes leads to failure.   Building an action culture does not mean promoting failure but instead creating clear rewards for success and for learning from failure.

Guideline 5: Fear creates rigidity.   Rigidity means an absence of action and an intolerance for change. If the path through uncertain, tough times is through experimentation and action, then fear must be expunged. This can be done only by engaging stakeholders in an inspirational mission and vision, rewarding success, and learning from failure.

Guideline 6: Collaborate (inside) to compete (outside).   Recall the ride of Paul Revere profiled in the section on social capital. Through his collaboration with influential others, Revere had a profound positive impact on the future of the United States. Such cooperation among individuals within an organization best develops and leverages the benefits of their social capital.

Guideline 7: What gets measured is what gets done.   Tough times add their own baggage in terms of stress, uncertainty, and information overload. A set of simple rules or metrics that guide decision making will serve the strategy more effectively than a proliferation of measures and controls.

Guideline 8: Leaders need to walk the talk.   This brings our dialogue, like our eight areas of activity in tough times, full circle. Values that are not acted upon are not shared or followed. What is acted upon (whether desirable or not) will be shared, repeated, followed, and mimicked.

In conclusion, tough times are just that—tough. However, there is ample reason to expect that many firms will emerge from tough times with better resources and capabilities than many of their competitors. The difference between the post-recession haves and have-nots? Organizations where managers remind themselves and act on what we already know about managing people and relationships will likely build a strong foundation for future prosperity. Those that do not may still emerge intact but will be speedily outpaced by the performance of the more able new competitors.

Onward and upward!

References

1. http://www.starbucks.com/aboutus/pressdesc.asp?id=814, accessed 12/3/2008.

2. http://www.starbucks.com/aboutus/pressdesc.asp?id=818, accessed 12/11/2008.

3. http://www.starbucks.com/aboutus/pressdesc.asp?id=822, accessed 12/11/2008.

4. http://www.starbucks.com/aboutus/pressdesc.asp?id=962, accessed 12/11/2008.

5. http://money.aol.com/news/articles/_a/bbdp/citigroup-plans-a-leaner-future-cuts/247427, accessed 12/11/2008

6. Jim Collins (2001). *Good to Great: Why Some Companies Make the Leap . . . and Others Don't*, New York: Collins Business; Jim Collins and Jerry Porras (1997). *Built to Last: Successful Habits of Visionary Companies*, New York: Collins Business.

7. J. Pfeffer (2007). *What Were They Thinking? Unconventional Wisdom About Management*, Boston: Harvard Business School Press.

8. R.F. Dobbs, T. Karakolev, and F. Malige (2002). Learning to love recessions. *The McKinsey Quarterly Online Edition*, http://www.mckinseyquarterly.com/Learning_to_love_recessions_1197, June 2002, accessed 12/4/2008.

9. Tom Peters (1999). *The Circle of Innovation: You Can't Shrink Your Way to Greatness*, New York: Vintage Press.

10. http://www.maxgladwell.com/2008/11/innovation-or-extinction-the-new-economic-reality/, Max Gladwell, 11/21/2008, accessed 11/26/2008.

11. James O'Toole (1995). *Leading Change: Overcoming the Ideology of Comfort and the Tyranny of Custom*, San Francisco: Jossey-Bass Publishers.

12. James O'Toole (1998). *Leading Change: The Argument for Values-Based Leadership*, New York: Ballantine Books.

13. John Kotter and James Heskitt (1992). *Corporate Culture and Performance*, New York: The Free Press; Jim Collins and Jerry Porras (1997). *Built to Last: Successful Habits of Visionary Companies*, New York: Collins Business.

14. C.K. Bart, N. Bontis, and S. Taggar (2001). A model of the impact of mission statements on firm performance. *Management Decision*, 39(1): 19–35; C. K. Bart and M.C. Baetz (1998). The relationship between mission statements and firm performance: An exploratory study. *Journal of Management Studies*, 35: 823–853; Jim Collins and Jerry Porras (2004). *Built to Last: Successful Habits of Visionary Companies*, New York: Collins Business.

15. Richard O-Halloran and David O'Halloran (1999). *The Mission Primer: Four Steps to and Effective Mission Statement*, Richmond, VA: Mission Incorporated.

16. From Richard O-Halloran and David O'Halloran (1999). *The Mission Primer: Four Steps to and Effective Mission Statement*, Richmond, VA: Mission Incorporated, p. 5.

17. O'Halloran and O'Halloran summarized Gast's laws from his unpublished teaching notes.

18. http://www.mars.com/global/downloads/Who+we+are/mars_the_five_principles_of_mars.pdf, accessed 11/26/2008.

19. http://www.mars.com/global/Who+We+Are/The+5+Principles.htm, accessed 11/26/2008.

20. http://www.intel.com/intel/index.htm?iid=gg_about+intel_aboutintel, accessed 11/26/2008.

21. Jim Collins and Jerry Porras (1997). *Built to Last: Successful Habits of Visionary Companies*, New York: Collins Business.

22. http://www.gene.com/gene/about/corporate/growthstrategy/mission.html, accessed 11/26/2008.

23. http://www.chipotle.com, accessed 12/01/2008.

24. M.A. Carpenter and W.G. Sanders (2008). Chipotle—Fast food chic? Available at SSRN: http://ssrn.com/abstract=1309774, accessed 12/01/2008.

25. L. Keller-Johnson (2004). Projects and strategy. *Harvard Management Update*, June, pp. 3–5.

26. L. Keller-Johnson (2004). Projects and strategy. *Harvard Management Update*, June, pp. 3–5.

27. The seminal source for threat rigidity is B.M Staw, L.E. Sandelands, and J.E. Dutton (1981). Threat-rigidity effects in organizational behavior: A multilevel analysis. *Administrative Science Quarterly*, 26: 501–524. Also see R. Harrington, D. Lemak, and K.W. Kendall (2002). The threat rigidity thesis in newly formed teams; An empirical test. *Journal of Business and Management*, 8: 127–145.

28. R.M. Kanter (2003). The psychology of turnarounds. *Harvard Business Review*, June: 3–11.

29. Eisenhardt, K.M. (1989). Making fast strategic decisions in high-velocity environments. *Academy of Management Journal*, 32: 543–576.

30. Bartlett and Ghoshal introduced the notion of the "individualized corporation," where great companies are defined by purpose, process, and people. That notion is extended here to encompass current and future customers, as well as other key stakeholders. C. Bartlett and S. Ghoshal (1997). *The Individualized Corporation: A Fundamentally New Approach to Management*, New York: HarperPerennial Press.

31. A. Muniz, Jr., and T.C. O'Guinn (1995). Brand community and the sociology of brands, in Kim P. Corfman and John G. Lynch (eds). *Advances in Consumer Research*, 1996, Volume 23, Provo, UT: Association for Consumer Research, pp. 265–266.

32. Based on firsthand discussions with the Harley-Davidson management team.

33. R. Srinivasan, A. Rangaswamy, and G. Lilien (2005). Turning adversity into advantage: Does proactive marketing during a recession pay off? *International Journal of Research in Marketing*, 22: 2: 109–125.

34. Cited in R.S. Vaile, E.T. Grether, and Reavis Cox (1952). *Marketing in the American Economy*, New York: Ronald Press.

35. R. Srinivasan, A. Rangaswamy, and G. Lilien (2005). Turning adversity into advantage: Does proactive marketing during a recession pay off? *International Journal of Research in Marketing*, 22: 2: 109–125.

36. R. Srinivasan, A. Rangaswamy, and G. Lilien (2005). Turning adversity into advantage: Does proactive marketing during a recession pay off? *International Journal of Research in Marketing*, 22: 2: 109–125.

37. R. Srinivasan, A. Rangaswamy, and G. Lilien (2005). Turning adversity into advantage: Does proactive marketing during a recession pay off? *International Journal of Research in Marketing*, 22: 2: 109–125.

38. http://www.kimwarren.com/2008/11/strategy-in-tough-times/, Kim Warren, 11/6/2008, accessed 12/2/2008.

39. http://www.betanews.com/article/Dell_Acquires_Alienware/1143070457, Ed Oswald, 3/26/2006, accessed 12/2/2008.

40. G. McWilliams (2004). Minding the store: Analyzing customers, Best Buy decides not all are welcome, *The Wall Street Journal*, November 8: A1.

41. L. Selden and G. Colvin (2003). *Angel Customers & Demon Customers*, New York: Penguin Group.

42. J. Pfeffer and R. Sutton (2006). *Hard Facts, Dangerous Half-Truths, and Total Nonsense: Profiting from Evidence-Based Management*, Boston: Harvard Business School Press.

43. J. Pfeffer and R. Sutton (2006). *Hard Facts, Dangerous Half-Truths, and Total Nonsense: Profiting from Evidence-Based Management*, Boston: Harvard Business School Press, p. 21.

44. http://www.kimwarren.com/2008/11/strategy-in-tough-times/Kim Warren, 11/6/2008, accessed 12/2/2008.

45. W. Cascio (1993). Downsizing: What do we know? What have we learned? *Academy of Management Executive*, 7: 95–104.

46. V. Chang, J. Chatman, and C. O'Reilly (2005). Developing a human capital strategy. *California Management Review*, 47: 137–167.

47. A great summary and history of lean is provided by J.P. Womack , D.T. Jones, and D. Roos (1991). *The Machine That Changed the World: The Story of Lean Production*, New York: HarperPerennial.

48. M. Kilduff and W. Tsai (2004). *Social Networks and Organizations*. London: Sage Publications, p. 2; M. Gladwell (2000). *The Tipping Point: How Little Things Can Make a Big Difference*. New York: Little Brown & Company.

49. R. Cross, S. Borgatti, and A. Parker (2002). Making invisible work visible, *California Management Review*, 44(2): 25–46.

50. This is a "kite" map (due to its shape), a social network concept popularized by Professor David Krackhart of Carnegie Mellon.

51. R. Cross, S. Borgatti, and A. Parker (2002). Making invisible work visible, *California Management Review*, 44(2): 25–46.

52. J. Barsh, M. Capozzi, and J. Davidson (2008). Leadership and innovation. *The McKinsey Quarterly*, January, pp. 37–47.

53. L. Fleming and M. Marx (2006). Managing creativity in small worlds. *California Management Review*, 48: 6–27.

54. R.S. Burt (2004). Structural holes and good ideas. *American Journal of Sociology*, 110: 349–399.

55. L. Fleming and M. Marx (2006). Managing creativity in small worlds. *California Management Review*, 48: 6–27.

56. P. Drucker (1993). *Management: Tasks, Responsibilities, and Practices*, New York: Collins Business.

57. J. Barsh, M. Capozzi, and J. Davidson (2008). Leadership and innovation. *The McKinsey Quarterly*, January, pp. 37–47.

58. W.C. Kim and R. Mauborgne (2005). Blue ocean strategy. *California Management Review*, 47: 3: 105–121.

59. M.A. Carpenter and W.G. Sanders (2009). *Strategic Management: A Dynamic Perspective*, Upper Saddle River, NJ: Pearson/Prentice Hall.

60. http://www.mckinseyquarterly.com/Innovative_management_A_conversation_between_Gary_Hamel_and_Lowell_Bryan_2065, J. Burish, 11/2007, accessed 12/4/2008.

61. M.A. Carpenter and W.G. Sanders (2009). *Strategic Management: A Dynamic Perspective*, Upper Saddle River, NJ: Pearson/Prentice Hall.

62. http://www.mckinseyquarterly.com/Innovative_management_A_conversation_between_Gary_Hamel_and_Lowell_Bryan_2065, J. Burish, 11/2007, accessed 12/4/2008.

63. http://www.mckinseyquarterly.com/Innovative_management_A_conversation_between_Gary_Hamel_and_Lowell_Bryan_2065, J. Burish, 11/2007, accessed 12/4/2008.

64. R. Kaplan and D. Norton (2001). *The Strategy Focused Organization*. Boston: HBS Press.

65. L. Gary (2002). How to think about performance measures now. *Harvard Management Update*, February, pp. 3–6.

66. R. Kaplan and D. Norton (2001). *The Strategy Focused Organization*. Boston: HBS Press.

67. L. Gary (2002). How to think about performance measures now. *Harvard Management Update*, February, pp. 3–6.

68. L. Gary (2002). How to think about performance measures now. *Harvard Management Update*, February, pp. 3–6.

69. R. Barrett (2006). *Building a Values-Driven Organization: A Whole System Approach to Cultural Transformation*, New York: Butterworth-Heinemann. These levels are analogous to, but more fine-grained than Covey's five levels of leadership.

70. http://www.valuescentre.com/docs/ValuesBasedLeadership.pdf, accessed 12/4/2008.

71. http://knowledge.emory.edu/article.cfm?articleid=774, C. Tycho Howle, 6/02/04, accessed 11/26/2008.

72. J. Pfeffer and R. Sutton (2000). *The Knowing–Doing Gap: How Smart Companies Turn Knowledge into Action*, Boston: Harvard Business School Press, p. ix.

73. T. Peters and R. Waterman (1982). *In Search of Excellence: Lessons from America's Best-Run Companies*, New York: Harper & Row.